God bless you!
Rhonda

RHONDA SCIORTINO

SUCCEED

because of what you've been

THROUGH

learn how to acquire the five points of prosperity

First Printing: February 2011

ISBN: 978-0-9830921-0-0

Library of Congress Control Number: 2010943411

Published by: N&SMG, Inc., P.O. Box 13175, Newport Beach, CA 92658

www.rhondasciortino.com

Printed in China

Cover & Interior Design: David Riley Associates
Newport Beach, CA
www.rileydra.com

Cover Photography: Svoboda Studios

DEDICATION

This book is dedicated to all the people who loved me when I was very difficult to love.

You loved me into wholeness, and as a result, I'm now able to truly love others.

You know who you are. God bless you.

If I hurt or offended you when I was one of the "walking wounded," please accept my sincere apology.

A SPECIAL NOTE TO NICK AND SARAH ...

I wouldn't be the person I've become if it weren't for you.

May God bless you both as much as you've blessed me.

ACKNOWLEDGEMENTS

There's no way to specifically name all the people who have played an important role in my life or even those who had some influence on the success I've enjoyed. There were teachers and school counselors, foster parents who took me in and introduced me to Jesus, people who befriended me, mentors, employers, co-workers, and the people I've been blessed to have closest to me. There were also those who mistreated me. I'm grateful to all of them.

Most of all I'm grateful to God for the amazing arrangements He made for me, for the opportunities He provided, and for giving me the strength to endure and the ability to see His hand in it all.

Although my childhood was full of negativity, there are three areas for which I give credit to the people who raised me. I'm grateful to my maternal grandparents (both now deceased) for taking me in. They didn't have to do it. Their motives were immaterial, and the quality of the care they provided is no longer relevant. The point is that after their two children were grown and gone, they started over raising their daughter's baby.

These people who beat me for any reason or no reason at all, gave me black eyes, burned me, and terrorized me in ways it's difficult for me to talk about even now are the same people who taught me to read before I was 4 years old and made me read from the dictionary and encyclopedia every day thereafter for the next twelve years. I'm grateful for the importance they placed on reading, for the escape my books provided, and for the perspective I have now because of the forced reading of my childhood.

The third thing for which I'm grateful to my grandparents is that, except for my brief time in a foster home and the times we were homeless, we lived in the same small, filthy, rodent and insect-infested shack. As awful as it was, it was consistent. In hindsight, that consistency provided a stability that helped maintain my sanity.

All of us have different "life assignments" and different talents and abilities that are perfectly matched to us. God's plan for your life may look very different from mine, and the benefits of living out His plan for your life may be quite different, but there are certain things that are true for all of us. First, God is the same yesterday, today, and forever. Second, He is not a respecter of persons. As a result of these two facts, we can count on God's love, mercy, and wisdom now just the same as at any other time in history; and God's power will work for anyone who will be bold enough to believe that He IS, that He is able, and that He desires to help us.

The transformation in me and every aspect of my life is nothing short of miraculous. I hope that reading about my metamorphosis will encourage and inspire you. Regardless of what your life currently looks like or what your Assignment may be, if you will incorporate the timeless principles included here into your life, like the law of gravity that works for everyone who tries it, these principles WILL work for you.

C O N T E N T S

For we are God's handiwork [unique creation or recipe], created in Christ Jesus to do good works, which God prepared in advance for us to do.

– God, as recorded in the Holy Bible in Ephesians 2:10

WHY WRITE IT NOW? MORE IMPORTANTLY, WHY READ IT?

I have a wonderful life. It's complete with family and friends who are wonderful, loyal, and fun. I have a rewarding career that allows me to work with the best people in the world – people who are committed to helping children who've been abused, molested, neglected, and abandoned. I live in a wonderful home on a hill overlooking the ocean. I drive cars that I never imagined riding in, much less owning; I travel anywhere I want to go; I can buy just about anything I desire; and I can help people in ways I never would have dreamed possible.

"That's all very nice," you say. *"But what's the big deal? You're not the only one living in those circumstances."* True. There are many successful entrepreneurs, and there are many "rags to riches" stories; after all, we live in the United States of America, the land of opportunity.

The *"big deal"* is that I went from welfare to wealth, from abandonment to an embracing family, from hunger to having more than enough food, from isolation to a network of solid relationships with people of integrity who can be counted on even in the most difficult of circumstances. I went from a hostile environment to one of peace, from constant tension and worry to a life of relaxed satisfaction. I went from having an inherited belief system of distortions and bigotry to setting a foundation of ethics and morals based on absolute truth. And I went from having less than nothing – no money, nothing to eat, no safe place to hide, no family, and no resources – to a level of prosperity that has, at times, been embarrassing in its apparent excess.

I was smart, but not the smartest. I wasn't hideous, but I was certainly not the most attractive. I was not athletic at all, nor the most educated, nor the best in any category. In fact, you could say that I had no breaks at all other than, perhaps, being white. Although my nearly transparent Caucasian skin was anything but an asset while growing up as the only white kid in my neighborhood, I expect it would have been doubly difficult in the workplace had I been covered in a different color skin.

How did I go from abandonment, poverty, and abuse to becoming a multi-millionaire? I'll give you a hint and say that it wasn't because I won the lottery or married a wealthy man. Both my husband and I eventually did become financially successful in our own separate businesses, but when we married, we were both still working very hard toward making our goals a reality – which at the time seemed like light years away.

My businesses and investments have generated significant profit through the years, but it hasn't happened suddenly, and it has nothing to do with luck, coincidence, being at the right place at the right time, or knowing the "right" people. My life changed as a result of implementing the principles that are the undercurrent of the story told here. Those principles, as well as the practical steps to apply them, will work for you. I am not saying it's the "only" way, but I am saying it is one way that has been proven to work.

I decided to write this book when I noticed so many people struggling in their relationships and finances. It occurred to me that perhaps sharing my perspective on established concepts and my experience in implementing these ideas could be just the key that unlocks the psychological padlocks of some who are trapped in a life of desperation or mediocrity as a result of adversity. Hopefully, when I communicate where I came from, where I am today, and what principles worked for me, I can make a difference in your life or that of someone you care about.

...as long as you are breathing,
you are capable of so much.

Many people throughout history have overcome adversity and gone from "rags to riches" by using the ideas included here. So why write another "how to" or motivational book on success? Well, imagine you hear a new song on the radio that you really like. No new notes were discovered or invented to create that music. The artist used the same notes that have been used in every piece of music since humans began humming, but a new combination of notes comes together to create a fresh, innovative song that sounds different than anything you've heard before. In the same way, I am hoping that I have been able to combine my experiences, education, and advice to create a fresh, distinctive story that will help you see that as long as you are breathing, you are capable of so much. You have within you the potential, and in your hands the proven strategies, to convert your potential into reality.

I was 27 years old before I told anyone that my parents had abandoned me. Of course my friends noticed that there were no parents around, but when questions arose, I would briefly mention their busy lives rather than tell the shameful truth that they didn't want me. Then I would change the subject as quickly as possible. The truth no longer stings; in fact, after all these years, what I'm about to tell you carries no emotion for me. It's as though I'm talking about someone I knew a long time ago and can only vaguely remember.

I never planned to tell anyone about my childhood, much less write a book, talk about it on television, and speak to groups of total strangers! I couldn't imagine the point of reliving an ugly past. I've left out the names of my biological parents, but should they read this and identify themselves on these pages, I hope they won't feel bad. I've totally forgiven them. I harbor no anger, bitterness, or resentment toward them, and I don't want them to feel any guilt about what happened all those years ago. They've probably carried around a lifetime of guilt. Nothing can be gained by adding to that.

This is not a book filled with the story of shocking, gory child abuse that resulted in a lifetime of misery. There are too many of those already. It has been reported that one in four girls and one in six boys are sexually abused. That's a huge number of people who are walking around wounded. There are far too many vulnerable children being abused by family or others while the adults in their lives aren't paying attention. Their stories are heartrending and difficult to read, and tragically, some victims of child abuse don't live to have the opportunity to tell their stories.

Despite the dramatic stories that have been publicized through print and in movies, the majority of victims of child abuse, neglect, abandonment, or molestation go on quietly with their lives, hoping that no one will pick the scabs off of their barely concealed wounds.

Often, the fractured memories of their painful experiences lie just below the surface and often trigger anger, frustration, or depression, leaving others wondering why they are overreacting.

What I hope to accomplish with this book is:

- To emphasize that we each create our own outcomes – good or bad. The principles included here will help you intentionally create good results.
- To encourage people living with abuse or other disadvantages to believe that they can get through it.
- To raise awareness that all people who have been abused do not turn out to be criminals, child abusers, or losers. In fact, survivors of abuse are everywhere. We are business owners, attorneys, physicians, contractors, judges, and insurance brokers. We work in every profession and live in every neighborhood. We are your co-workers, friends, and neighbors, and we could wind up marrying into your family!
- To tell employers that many who have experienced adversity make excellent employees if given the opportunity, guidance, and patience. Because of the unfairness that we could not control and the bad choices and behaviors that almost inevitably follow in our efforts to control what we can, we often come across as difficult or belligerent as we struggle to protect ourselves from being hurt again. The good news is that we are often motivated to break through the limitations and exceed the expectations set by and for us. **Not despite, but because of** abuse, neglect, abandonment, or other unfair circumstances, many of us are driven by a force more powerful than any motivation an employer can conjure up. It's the desire to be wanted and valued, to do something worthwhile, to fit in, to be approved of, to be liked, and to have all the things that were denied to us when we had no control over our circumstances. Not just

tangible things like houses and cars, but the intangibles like good relationships, security, the feeling of a warm, comfortable bed and the ability to sleep peacefully in the absence of fear. Many of us are highly motivated to reach for the self-worth and dignity that comes only from an earned paycheck.

So, why read this book? To reach for and create a better life for yourself. I've included here what I believe is necessary to achieve financial prosperity and, more importantly, good relationships, health, hope, and the incomparable satisfaction that comes from finding and fulfilling your purpose. After you read about where I came from and the path I took to arrive at my present life, I hope that you'll know that you, too, can do what I did and achieve the same or better results.

And just in case you're tempted to say that it's too late or it doesn't matter – as long as you're still breathing (and I assume you are as you read this book), there is still an opportunity to change your circumstances. You might be amazed at what can happen, sometimes in a relatively short period of time, when you implement principles that have worked for many successful people, including this former "white trash ghetto girl."

It won't cost you anything but some time away from the television or computer to read this book and learn how you can make your life what you want it to be. Really think about the way you're spending your life. Are you spending your free time in front of the television, playing video games, hanging out with friends, drinking, doing drugs, or just wasting your time on things that aren't moving you toward a better future? You can _spend_ your time doing whatever you choose to do. Or, you can _invest_ your time in reading this book, implementing its suggestions, feeling good about moving toward your goals, and celebrating as you achieve them.

Either way, five years from now you'll be five years older. You can either be five years older doing the same things you're doing now, with the same difficulties and same unsatisfying results, OR you can be five years older living in the house you want to live in, driving the car you want to drive, doing what you want to do, and feeling really good about your life. It's your choice.

Whatever adversity you've experienced is what qualifies
you to fulfill your specific purpose.

If you implement the suggestions in this book or in any other proven plan for success, and people around you ridicule or criticize you, consider their lives. Are they living an awesome life like the one you'd like to have? If not, they are not qualified to have an opinion that "counts" in your life. Throw their opinions and criticisms out with the trash and move toward your future. I guarantee you, when you have all you want to have and are living the life you want to live, they'll either still be criticizing you (only this time out of jealousy), or they'll be asking for your advice on how to turn their lives around!

The book in your hands will help you understand what you have to do to create a successful life and to see yourself in a way that you may never have before – as a skilled, talented, educated adult able to handle circumstances that would knock most people down and maybe out. Whatever adversity you've experienced is what qualifies you to fulfill your specific purpose.

CHAPTER 1

LESSONS FROM ABUSE

I don't know how to explain how very different my life is today without describing how it used to be. I want it to be very clear that I went from being a ward of the court to where I am today *without winning the lottery, marrying a wealthy man, or inheriting anything other than trash – literally.*

In December of 1961, my mother gave a package to the neighbor, but it wasn't a Christmas gift. It was me, her six-month-old baby girl. Hours after the diapers and formula had been used up, my mother still hadn't returned from her shopping trip. The neighbor was nervous that something terrible had happened – and if there hadn't been some tragedy, she was upset that this woman had really stretched the limits of their friendship by burdening her with a baby and absolutely no communication about this extended absence.

When there was still no word by the next morning, the neighbor called my mother's mother. My grandmother lived with her physically abusive husband, my grandfather, in filth and poverty. She numbed her pain with alcohol, but she never worked up the courage to do anything to change her circumstances. When my grandmother got that call from the neighbor, she came to get me, thinking she'd keep the baby until her daughter showed up. It didn't occur to my grandmother then that, like so many grandparents, she was starting over by raising another child.

Days and weeks passed with no word from my mother. There were no reports of any car accidents. No local hospital had admitted anyone by her name. None of her friends knew where she was, or if they knew, they weren't talking. My father was working seven days a week as a truck driver, so no one could reach him to ask if he had any idea where his wife had run off to this time. Months passed before anyone learned that my mother had met a guy who she thought could give her the life she longed for. When she told the neighbor she was going shopping, she was already packed and ready to move out of state with him.

That December day was the start of the most fearful and painful sixteen years of my life. But before you go feeling pity for the little girl I used to be, consider the fact that those horrendous experiences provided an education I couldn't get any other way. Those sixteen years formed an unshakeable foundation on which I launched a lifetime of determining *what works* to improve the circumstances we find ourselves in, whether they result from our own poor choices or were forcibly imposed on us.

Except for a very brief time in a foster home and the months that we were homeless, during those sixteen years I lived in a filthy, rodent and insect-infested environment filled with strange and superstitious beliefs. The dilapidated 500-square-foot house we lived in was built in the early 1900's, had no heating other than the burners on top of the gas stove, and certainly had no air conditioning. We used a *"full"* toilet that was flushed only when *"absolutely necessary"* by pouring a bucket of water into it. This drained into a cesspool that frequently overflowed, its contents running down the driveway and out into the street where the neighborhood children played. As a result of the cesspool situation, I bathed only weekly in about an inch of water and went months without washing my hair. Until I was 13, I didn't own a toothbrush. Until I went to high school, I had no idea that people showered, brushed their teeth, and washed their hair EVERY DAY!

What can you do to change your circumstances?

I wore clothes and shoes that we bought at the thrift store or picked out of the local dump. My clothes were ill-fitting and out of style, and my feet usually hurt from being squeezed into shoes that were too small. But kids making fun of the way I looked and sore feet were the least of my problems.

To say that the house was disgusting was an understatement. The grime from the five to six packs of cigarettes smoked there every day clung to the walls; the slightest brush up against them left a gooey brown smudge on our clothing. The floor was wood, and I don't mean the beautiful hardwood that covers the floors of many lovely homes. I am referring to the plywood that held the bottom of that old house off the dirt over which it sat. There were holes through which mice, spiders, and assorted insects climbed in and out of the crawl space under the house to live off the spilled food and drinks that littered the kitchen floor. Some of the larger holes were "repaired" by nailing the tops of vegetable cans over them into the floor. Since we spent the summers barefoot, I learned early and often to navigate carefully around the "landmines" of the sharp can lids.

While Alice on *The Brady Bunch* was doing the family's laundry in an electric washer and dryer that were actually <u>inside</u> the house, we had a wringer washing machine outside on the back porch. If we had an exceptionally rainy season, there was no point in washing the clothes because there was no place to hang them to dry. So, there were many, many times when I not only wore the same jeans and shirt to school day after day, but I wore them dirty and reeking of the smell of body odor and cigarette smoke – so much smoke that my second grade teacher sent me to the principal's office for disciplinary action when I was 8 years old. I NEVER smoked! I hated cigarette smoke and the headaches and breathing difficulties that came with it; I still despise cigarette smoke and the way it makes me feel. But until I left that house at 16, I smelled of a toxic mixture of body odor, stale cigarettes, and occasionally alcohol after being hit with a glass or bottle of it.

The little house we lived in was hardly big enough for two, so there was no room for another bed. As implausible as it sounds, I slept in a crib in the corner of the room until I was 7 years old. When I could no longer curl up enough to fit in the crib, we hauled home an old twin mattress someone had left at the curb and put it on the closet floor. That little closet was my "room" until I was 16, and I was grateful for it. Even though it had no door, I was grateful to have that space because it was difficult for my grandfather to get inside. I could finally stretch all the way out in a place where I was off of the floor. I could turn my lamp on and read while my grandparents watched the blaring television on the other side of the plywood wall. For the first time in my life I could change clothes without anyone watching. In that little closet, it was easier to entertain the fantasy that I was like other kids.

Although we always eked out enough money for cigarettes and booze, we were often short on food. Above the sense of abandonment, the abuse, the neglect, and the craziness of that time of my life, my strongest memory was of the hunger.

From my earliest memories, I recall being put outside in the morning and not being allowed back in until nighttime. I remember feeling hungry as that front door closed behind me, wondering what I was going to eat that day. I'd take half-eaten meals out of trash cans, scrounge through the grocery dumpster for expired food, pick fruit and nuts off neighbors' trees, and show up at their houses at meal times, nervously hoping that they'd ask me to stay. My grandparents and I often went fishing in the nearby lake, sometimes until late into the evening, hoping to catch something for dinner. There were many times that we'd come home with only two or three small fish that we'd clean and cook late at night. It all seemed normal to me.

To say that the neighborhood we lived in was "rough" doesn't begin to describe it. The house next to ours was what we called a "way station" for illegal immigrants. While their forged papers were being created and they looked for jobs and a more permanent place to live, these people paid our neighbors to stay in their converted garage that housed three-bunk-tall cots lining each wall. The neighbors who lived in the house subsidized their income from this "papers" business by growing and selling marijuana.

Next to that house lived a family whose father and oldest son committed a drive-by shooting, killing the mother of a young man who had "dumped" our neighbor's daughter for another girl. The house next to them was occupied by a Hell's Angels motorcycle gang. You get the picture. In my neighborhood there weren't any homeowner association meetings or summer barbeques where people brought their favorite potato salad.

I was hyper vigilant the entire time I lived in that house, and it resulted in a diagnosis of migraine headaches and an ulcer when I was 14. But the state of "high alert" I lived in wasn't entirely due to the scary neighbors around our little house. It was because of the mentally ill man and the alcoholic woman inside! In addition to the filth, the poverty, the hunger, the terrible smell of the overflowing cesspool, and the dirty, ill-fitting clothes, there was the *craziness*. There is really no more appropriate word for it.

Convinced that some kind of revolt and government overthrow were imminent, my grandfather was determined that I be prepared. So, when I was 4 years old, he began training me in the care and use of firearms, taking me to remote areas of California, like Lytle Creek and Apple Valley, for target practice. He taught me how to use my peripheral vision to assess people for their level of potential threat without ever making eye contact. He taught me how to walk boldly through a dicey area by holding my posture erect and confidently acting (the keyword here is *acting*) as though I belonged there just as much, if not more, than anyone else.

My grandfather taught me that I should carry a weapon, but never, under any circumstances, should I tell anyone I had it or threaten someone with it. If I pulled it out of concealment, I was to use it. If I used it, I was to aim for the heart. Never wound. Always kill. When I was 4, he'd tell me that I was so inaccurate with my shooting that I'd aim for the heart and, if I was lucky, hit the victim's big toe. By the time he completed my training, he joked that if I had a chance to pull and aim, I better be prepared to describe in detail the way it all went down because the other guy wouldn't be giving any testimony. While other people were proud of their child's performance in softball or dance, my grandfather was proud of my ability to take aim and accurately shoot, followed by taking apart, cleaning, and reassembling my firearm in acceptable time.

One would have thought my grandfather was highly skilled in the area of espionage or some high level military or law enforcement unit. In fact, he was a security guard following a brief stint in the Navy from which he was prematurely discharged, a topic which was never discussed.

I am aware of how nutty this all sounds. But the truth is that before I started kindergarten, leaving the house on my own for the first time, I was taught that should someone try to attack me on the way home, I was not to turn and defend myself, but to run as fast as I could while at the same time trying to lure the attacker into my house. I was taught that I only had to make it through the front door because there were loaded, ready weapons in various places throughout the little house, including right inside the front door. It was made clear to me that it would be not only acceptable but commendable if I were able to grab a weapon and shoot the attackers upon luring them home. The only condition was that I must wait until they had at least one foot inside the door before firing the first shot.

I didn't carry a gun to and from school. I was given a switchblade for that. All those things that this madman taught me helped me boldly strut past every potential threat for the two-mile walk to and from school, from kindergarten until the day I emancipated. I didn't say I walked "fearlessly." I was scared to death on a fairly consistent basis, but you would never have known it.

Living in this house taught me an extremely valuable lesson. If you're afraid, then do what you have to do while being afraid, and never allow anyone who could take advantage of your weakness know you're afraid. And never allow anyone or any circumstance to intimidate you to the point that you shut down and do nothing. Just do it afraid. The more I did what I had to do, the more I was capable of protecting myself and, ultimately, the more confidence I had in my ability to do whatever I had to do.

Unfortunately, all that I learned to protect myself outside the house did little for me inside the house. When I was 4 years old, I had a skillet of hot oil thrown at me, allegedly because I wouldn't be quiet. I had cigarettes ground out in the nearest limb when my grandparents were looking for an outlet for their anger. The man who used to say, "No *one will ever hurt you as long as I'm alive,"* was the man who gave me all my black eyes.

My grandfather was 6'2", wore his dark hair slicked back, and carefully groomed a thin mustache that reminded me of the pictures I'd seen of a young Howard Hughes. Even in his fifties, he was still an attractive man – except when he smiled. Then he was frightening – partly because the teeth that hadn't already fallen out had rotted and were mostly brownish black and green. Mostly though, the fear I felt was directly tied to his black eyes that would narrow to just slits when he smiled, the same way they did when he was screaming. He reminded me of something evil that jumped out at the "good guy" in horror movies. The scariest part of being around him was that he was totally unpredictable.

My grandfather quit his jobs or got himself fired from them on a fairly regular basis. Typically this was because he'd throw a punch at his boss, steal merchandise (*while working as a security guard, no less*), or simply decide his employers weren't paying him enough, and he'd just decide not to go to work. My grandmother never did offer to work. She preferred to spend her days reading romance novels, watching soap operas, playing with an Ouija board, and drinking until she passed out.

Having said all this, I have to add that there were some bright spots in my childhood. Every day from my earliest memories, my grandfather would say to me, "*You don't know anything important.*" While this sounds offensive, that was his cue for me to tell him what I'd learned that day. I knew he was challenging me to learn something meaningful every day. Child rearing specialists might frown on his approach, but it was very effective motivation for me

24

since I was so eager to please this impossible-to-please man.

What I wanted was to hold my own in conversation with my grandfather. Consequently, I read the newspaper every day, watched the news every night, read *U.S. News & World Report* from cover to cover every week, read from the encyclopedia every day, and checked the dictionary for the many words I was learning along the way so that I'd be ready for him. I'd wait, sometimes all evening, for him to say it. When he walked through the door, I'd be ready, bursting at the seams and eager to tell all. I suspect that he got a kick out of making me think he'd forgotten and making me wait him out. And when he'd finally say, *"You don't know anything important,"* I'd enthusiastically yell, *"OH YES I DO!"* And I'd proceed to tell excitedly of the "important thing" I knew.

He'd sit and listen to me, ask questions, sometimes challenge my understanding of the "important thing," tell me where I'd gotten it wrong, or just accept the information. I don't remember him ever saying that I did a good job, or anything like that, but it didn't matter. I didn't even know positive affirmation was missing in my life until I was exposed to a family where the kids were praised for a job well done.

Perhaps the brightest spot of my childhood years was the time when I was placed with what I later realized was a foster family. My memories of that brief time are vague. I don't recall their names, the city we were in, or how long I was there. The memories of that time feel now, so many years later, like the foggy remembrances of a dream. I recall the clean house, the white linoleum kitchen floor (I was very impressed with that clean, white floor), and the way in which those people spoke to each other and to me. It was the first time in my life that I felt completely safe. I could change clothes behind closed doors. I felt clean. I slept on soft, clean sheets. I had plenty to eat.

Those people influenced my life in three profound ways. First, they took me to church and introduced me to Jesus. This was the first time that the concept of a "loving Father" had been introduced to me. Of course it was an abstract concept that I didn't understand, but the seed had been planted. Second, they exposed me to a way of living that was completely foreign to me. They resolved conflict by discussion. There were no raised voices or fists flying. Third, the one and only thing I recall either of them saying to me was something that changed my life – but not until over twenty years later.

Although I remember so little else, I recall sitting on that white kitchen floor crying. I have no idea why, but I suppose that as a little girl separated from everything she'd ever known, I was feeling unsettled and scared. The foster father stood over me and in a strong tone said, "You better quit feeling sorry for yourself. You were put here for a reason, and you better be about finding out what it is." I was stunned and very maturely screamed in my little girl voice, "I HATE YOU!"

It wasn't long after that day that I was removed from that home and placed back into the abusive environment with my grandparents. I learned that my grandfather had filed a complaint against the foster parents for having taken me to church and trying to indoctrinate me with their religious fantasies. I lived the balance of my first sixteen years in abuse, but the positive influence of those foster parents remains tangible in my life to this day. As a result of that one interaction many years ago, I am focused on fulfilling my life purpose, which is to help others who have been victimized to identify and embrace their strengths and to fulfill their unique purpose for living.

The "craziness" in which I was raised was awful, but it seemed normal to me at the time. Through the years of reading newspapers and magazines, seeing things on television that were very different from the way we lived, having been exposed to that foster family, and being exposed to teachers and students who were good people from much healthier environments, I began to see that what I knew as normal was not quite so. I began to have hope for something better – I just didn't know how to get to it. Had I not read as I did, I might have continued to think that everything about the way we lived and the ugly circumstances and negative attitudes were normal. That's how anger, depression, failure to take responsibility for our actions, failure to act, mistreatment of children, and many other negative things get perpetuated from generation to generation. For those of us who have experienced adversity, "normalcy" must be created deliberately. To do that, we have to look at the lives of people who have the kind of life we want to live and emulate them.

...look at the lives of people who have the kind of life you want to live.

My father knew about the condition of the house and the people I lived with (since my grandparents had been his in-laws), but he never called to check on me. Even though he lived only ten miles away, he came by only once a year, on Christmas Eve, to see how I was doing (but by the time I was 8, those visits stopped too). And although I fantasized throughout my whole childhood about my father rescuing me, it never happened. He had remarried, lived in a nice house in a nice community, had started a new life, and didn't want to be reminded of the mistakes of his past.

My mother, who not only knew of the conditions I lived in but had grown up in the same house and been reared by the same abusive people, never did come back for me. I have seen her a total of six times in my life, and she never, on any of those occasions, offered to rescue me or even encouraged any ongoing relationship with me. She had remarried and had two other children after me, whom she kept and raised in a custom-built, tri-level home on a lake in a nice community. She, like my father, had started a new life, and didn't want to be burdened with the responsibilities that went along with the mistakes of her past.

After many years of thinking that one of these two people was going to show up one day and sweep me out of that house and on to a wonderful life, I finally realized that if I were going to make it out of there alive, I was going to be the one to figure out how to do it. No one would come to rescue me. Some of the things I did and decisions I made likely make no sense to people who came from a decent family. But others who, like me, were looking for opportunities to create a better life for themselves will likely understand completely, and perhaps they will even see their own story reflected in mine.

You can deliberately create a great life!

Raised as I was, I didn't have high (or even average) expectations or "minimum requirements" on what I would accept in terms of the way others treated me. I was so desperate to have someone care about me that I regularly gave my lunch to a girl in the neighborhood in exchange for being allowed to play with her and her friends. When I was 13, I literally and figuratively dove into the arms and the passenger seat of the first guy who showed an interest in me. I married at 17, a year after I emancipated, had a baby, and was divorced by the time I was 21.

I was 27 years old before I admitted to anyone that I had been a ward of the court, and even then there was no way I was going to tell people any details about what I'd experienced. I was ashamed of the fact that my parents didn't want me. On some level, I thought that if people knew the truth, they wouldn't want me around either. When many of us coming out of dysfunctional or abusive environments finally escape them, we don't care to tell anyone about the pain and the shame. We had to live this life, and we don't want to relive it again and again by having people ask questions about our experiences. And we surely don't want to be vulnerable to people who might use that very intimate information to hurt us.

While my story includes abandonment, abuse, neglect, and poverty, the core of it, and that of many other people who had at least one parent who was *missing in action*, is really about feeling unwanted. My earliest experiences influenced my perceptions of reality and the motives of people. I wanted to know why bad things happen to innocent, vulnerable people. Why was I alive? Was there a God? If so, what the heck was He doing while the weaker, smaller, and more vulnerable of us were being hurt by the bigger, stronger ones? How could I protect myself and get out of this alive? And the question that really burned inside of me, although I probably couldn't have verbalized it until much later, was this: What could I do to change my circumstances?

There is no point in sensationalizing the story by talking about details of abuse that happened years ago. Every one of us has a story. Mine is no more poignant than anyone else's. Everyone's pain is significant to them. What is important for anyone who wants a better life is to know that we each can deliberately create a great life regardless of how it started or where we are now.

CHAPTER 2

LESSONS FROM OTHERS

All of us pay our dues in one way or another. No one achieves complete prosperity of *health, joy, peace, good relationships, and financial stability,* and everything that goes along with all that, without paying his or her dues. And I was no exception.

You may be able to think of a few people who *seem* to have become successful without paying their dues. I guarantee that there is no shortcut to the real success that includes the five key components of prosperity that I've listed above. Money is a great tool to keep you warm, fed, and comfortable, but it can't keep you from being miserable and lonely. The best type of financial prosperity comes along as part of the entire package.

The biggest return on my years of paying dues came from learning everything I could in every situation. Hopefully, we have all learned – for good or bad – from the circumstances of our upbringings. Sometimes we are not even consciously aware of the conclusions we have drawn. It is important to figure out what we have learned in life, so that we can sort through and get rid of those things that no longer serve us or make no sense.

For example, I learned from watching the alcoholic woman who raised me that I would not tolerate anything that even resembled abuse from a man because I did NOT want to be like her. I was disgusted by her weakness and acceptance of the abuse she and I both suffered, along with her failure to even try to protect us, and I was determined to never be weak and timid.

I learned a lot from that crazy man who raised me. Much of it has been reevaluated and tempered or dismissed over the years, but all of it factored into who I am today. For example, he controlled the foods we were allowed to eat, and punished us by withholding food. From that feeling of powerlessness and the awful hunger that I so often felt came my determination to work and earn my own money so that I could always buy my own food. And should the need arise, I could leave an abusive situation immediately and still survive.

Other things reevaluated and discarded are the beliefs that all romance novels are bad, people with red hair are mean, and men who wear pinky rings should not be trusted. I am aware that these things sound silly, but I include them here to make the point that some of us are carrying around beliefs and prejudices that were planted in our minds as young children when we didn't have the ability to consider the validity of the assertion or its source. I've changed my thoughts on many conclusions drawn from the observations of a child in a dysfunctional environment who didn't have the benefit of the whole picture and the maturity to assess it all. Most of us who had a less than ideal upbringing could benefit from reconsidering many of the assumptions we formed as children.

Fortunately, I had some great school teachers who took a genuine interest in me and taught me skills that I used to change my life.

If I'd grown up in a rural area or some place where all the kids in school were in similar circumstances, it wouldn't have been so difficult. But at Upland High School this was not the case. I quickly learned that my experience of being a Southern Californian was distinctly different from that of most others. And because my clothes were always worn, out of style, dirty, and reeking of cigarette smoke, I did all I could to blend in with the walls and desks and chairs.

Although those of us from the barrio attended Upland High School, the majority of the kids were from a nice, middle class area. The girls wore stylish clothes, had their hair styled, and had been Girl Scouts and soccer players (there was no money for uniforms and such for kids like me). Many were encouraged to participate in extra-curricular activities like cheerleading, which was also out of the question for me and others like me. Many students drove nice cars to school after they got their driver's licenses; in fact, some actually received shiny new Mustangs and Camaros on their 16th birthday. For my 16th birthday, I was hoping for a judge who would grant an emancipation order that would end the reign of terror in my life.

I did a fairly good job of learning as much as I could from every teacher right up until I met Mrs. Barbara Moyer in my freshman year of high school. Mrs. Moyer had a reputation for being one of the toughest teachers in my high school. I learned quickly that she deserved her reputation.

Despite my best efforts to blend into the background and make myself invisible, I found myself sitting in the back of Mrs. Moyer's freshman typing class with all eyes on me. She had walked all the way back to where I sat and was standing over me, pointing out to the entire class that I was looking at the typewriter keys. I was mortified, my stomach was tied in knots, I was sweating, and I was overwhelmed with a mixture of fear, anger, and humiliation. My hair was greasy. I was dirty. I smelled of BO. I couldn't believe that after having tried so hard to be transparent, every eye was on me. I could feel my cheeks getting hot and knew that, to add insult to injury, my face was bright red. I sat there not saying a word as she taped a piece of paper to the IBM Selectric typewriter and stood there while I tried to type, unable to see the keys. I had no idea where my fingers should start, and when she encouraged me to begin, the only thing that showed up on the paper was gibberish. She righted my fingers and I began again. I was grateful when she finally moved on.

In spite of this embarrassing experience, I later discovered that this teacher who I thought was unnecessarily cruel was actually one of the most genuinely concerned and gifted teachers I have ever known. She worked extra hard with me and had patience. She showed me how to feel the little bumps on the "f" and "j" keys so that I'd know where to place my fingers on home row. She encouraged me to practice typing at home. When I told her I had no typewriter at home, she didn't pity me and let me off the hook. She came up with a creative idea. She suggested that if I'd practice tapping out words on an "invisible typewriter" while others were talking or while I was watching television at night, it would establish the "qwerty" keyboard in my brain so that eventually I'd be able to type without even thinking about what I was typing. It worked. When I graduated from Upland High School, in addition to graduating in the top ten of my class, I held the record for fastest, most accurate typist – quite an achievement for someone who had no typewriter on which to practice outside of class.

Mrs. Barbara Moyer taught me more significant lessons. Because she spent extra time with me during her breaks and sometimes at lunch, I got to know her as a person. I knew that she was going through a really rough time and dealing with something that would have leveled most people. Both of her children had been abducted by their father. They had been gone for about two months, and she had no idea where they were or when she'd see them again. Amazingly, although she was going through this gut-wrenching personal ordeal, she came to school every day, gave 100% to all of her students, and never, ever neglected her teaching duties. I was one of a small group of people, and I think the only student, who knew what she was going through. I remember looking at her standing up in front of the class and teaching as though nothing was more important than that day's lesson. Wow! What a powerful lesson she taught me. That's when I first recognized what I later learned was work ethic. It was by emulating the work ethic I saw in her that I later achieved the success I was after.

Another thing I learned from her, although she didn't know it until twenty years after the fact, was that she unknowingly influenced me to become a Christian. She never proselytized or even mentioned God or religion in class, but when I asked her how she was able to function under her painful circumstances, she told me it was because of her faith in God. I asked her what that meant and where she got this faith. I listened as she talked about having a peace that was beyond all human understanding, and I thought, "*Well, it sure is beyond anything I can understand.*" What Mrs. Moyer didn't know was that as a result of her quiet testimony, I signed myself up for a class at the same church denomination that she attended, and shortly after my 15th birthday, I got baptized. I wanted – no, I needed – what she had. Of all that she contributed to my life, planting the seed of my current faith is the most important.

I was so impressed by Mrs. Moyer's work ethic, her even-tempered demeanor and her quiet, unshakable faith. Her ability to teach and motivate students enabled me to easily acquire the skills I would need to get a job and make a living. I'm still impressed.

One of the most wonderful gifts she gave me was to look me straight in the eyes when she spoke to me. Until Mrs. Moyer did this, I didn't realize that most people, including other teachers, looked quickly away from me. I don't know if it was because I was dirty, because I smelled, because they were turning away from the bruises they saw or the pain they perceived in my eyes, or simply because they were busy and had to move on to the next kid. It doesn't matter. She looked at me while she talked to me as though I were the most important person in the world at that moment. It's not as though she favored me. She did that for everyone. I watched her do it. Without saying a word, she taught me that one way to really honor people is to look them in the eyes when you speak to them. By that simple action, which she later told me she hadn't even been aware of doing, she gave me my very first sense of dignity. I liked it. And I wanted more of it.

Despite the humiliation at the beginning of our relationship, or perhaps because of it, Mrs. Barbara Moyer turned out to be the most influential teacher in my life. I mean no disrespect to my other good teachers, the school counselors, and the social workers I had in those first sixteen years. But if Mrs. Moyer at Upland High School hadn't pushed me as she did, I wouldn't have been motivated to master the shorthand, typing, and other office skills that were the specific reason that I was the applicant chosen for my first job, which ultimately led to my independence and played a very meaningful role in my success.

From the time I graduated until my own daughter went to Upland High School twenty years later, I had no communication with Mrs. Moyer. When I reconnected with her after all those years and told her what she'd done for me, she was shocked. She remembered me as a student, but had no recollection of the way I looked, and had never known of my circumstances.

CHAPTER 3

LESSONS AFTER I THOUGHT I KNEW EVERYTHING

I read somewhere that it was possible to become an emancipated minor, and I couldn't wait to apply for emancipation and to be on my own. Although my grandparents were against it, when I was 15, I applied, saw a judge, and was sent away with a long list of tasks I was to complete before I could return. That list included getting a job, finding an apartment I could afford, getting a driver's license, obtaining transportation, opening a checking account and a savings account, and maintaining good grades in high school.

After seeing the judge, I went directly to the ROP (Regional Occupational Program) office at Upland High School to see what kind of jobs they could find to help me. There were two available. One was a teller trainee at the local bank and the other was at a local insurance agency. "Great, I'll take the insurance interview. By the way, WHAT'S INSURANCE?" (More on that later.) I went to that interview and got that job. Now I had one requirement checked off of my list.

In order to meet the other requirements, I had to make more

money. So, in addition to the customer service and telemarketing job in that first insurance agency at age 15, I made extra money by tutoring other kids in English and algebra. I also worked nights and weekends in a shoe store, sold blankets that I knitted or crocheted, bathed stinky dogs at a kennel, and kept my eyes and ears open for opportunities to earn every additional dollar possible. Doing odd jobs for people to earn money wasn't new to me. I'd been finding ways to earn money since I was 6 years old. As early as I can remember, I instinctively knew that opportunities to make money always involved helping someone. If someone had a friend or knew a family who needed help with moving, cleaning, painting a house, pulling weeds, or whatever, I could be counted on to show up because I was always looking for opportunities to make extra income.

To the surprise of the judge, I returned shortly after my 16th birthday with proof that I had a job, a driver's license, a car *and its ownership certificate,* an apartment, and a checking and savings account. Thankfully, he granted my request for emancipation. It was official. I was an adult!

Somehow I thought that emancipating to adulthood would guarantee that no one would ever be able to get close enough to hurt me again. What a joke! There was still pain, plenty of it. While being emancipated did give me a sense of control over my life, the one thing that remained the same was that I felt so alone. There was no one to fall back on. No safety net. No one to call at 3:00 a.m. if I needed to go to the emergency room. No one who says, *"Call me when you get home to let me know you made it okay."* I'd hear parents of friends say things like this to their children, and I'd feel so sorry for myself because there wasn't anyone who cared if I made it home safely. There was no one to bail me out of a mess had I found myself in one – literally or figuratively. No family of my own to spend Christmas with. No one to loan me money if I couldn't buy groceries. If I needed something and couldn't afford it, I'd do without. I went without food plenty of times. But that wasn't difficult for me. That happened frequently when I was a kid. The difference was that once I had been granted emancipation, I knew that I was in control of my future.

What I know now that I didn't know in the self-pity of my adolescence is that there are many people who feel a deep sense of loneliness. Widows, divorcees, people in rest homes, people who had families who perished in an accident, and people who lost everything through natural disaster, crime, or some other circumstances completely beyond their control. There are those who committed a criminal act for which they're remorseful and have paid their time, but lost everyone and everything in the process. I could go on and on. I thought that "everyone else" had a great life. It didn't occur to me until much later that everyone experiences serious pain at some point in life.

I now know that it doesn't take much looking to find someone who is hurting. People all around us are dealing with an ugly medical diagnosis, a cheating spouse, financial problems, kids on drugs, and every other source of pain. What I know now that I didn't know then is that when people act like jerks, it probably has nothing to do with me. More likely, it's because of something they are dealing with or going through.

I recall as a child seeing the picture of John F. Kennedy, Jr. playing under his daddy's desk in the Oval Office. I wondered why I wasn't born to a daddy who loved me, or one who was amused by me, or even one who just tolerated me. Many of us had parents who left us, who were working all the time, or who were physically present but as distant as if they were on another planet as a result of being emotionally detached or influenced by drugs or alcohol.

Regardless of the dysfunctional family circumstances, the result is the same. It's the feeling of having been abandoned. What I'm saying is that this group of people who experienced some kind of dysfunction as children is a big club, and what we need to do is NOT feel sorry for ourselves but CHOOSE to feel grateful for the opportunity we have now to change our circumstances and to help others change theirs.

Do not feel sorry for yourself.

What people who were born into loving families find difficult to understand is this: When it is clear that you were unwanted, there is a prevailing sense of being worthless that permeates everything. The feeling of being unwanted is not limited to those original people who didn't want you. It feels like an ugly sweater that you're forced to wear everywhere. You automatically think that everyone you meet will regard you as unwanted and not valuable before a word is ever said to you. The vague feeling of being worthless influences all decisions, all relationships, and perhaps more importantly, all actions and failures to act.

I say all this not to evoke sympathy, but to illustrate that I know what it is to have absolutely no self-esteem, no job experience, no appropriate attire, and nearly no social skills and still muster up the courage to do things like go to a job interview.

Had I not known how to type and had I not worked up the courage to go on that first job interview, I never would have gotten the job in that insurance agency, which led to approval of my emancipation request and ultimately to my lifelong career in the insurance industry. Had I not known shorthand, I wouldn't have been hired by a local homeowner association to take the minutes of their meetings. Had I not been in on those meetings, I wouldn't have been exposed to real estate, and I may not have been motivated to buy my first house when I was 18 and later generate millions of dollars in profit from investments.

I was grateful to the man who gave me that first job, but in order to make more money, I needed more hours than were available there. So I subsequently took three different insurance agency jobs on my way to the one in which I stayed for nearly seven years.

I left the first of those three jobs because the agency owner, a married man and father of four, would get down on one knee next to my desk and sing to me. He was probably harmless, but I was so uncomfortable, turning bright red as he'd sing the same song lyric each time, *"I'm in the mood for love simply because you're near me."*

At the next insurance agency, my boss, who was an amateur body builder, picked me up, chair and all, and threatened to drop me when I wouldn't respond to his sexual advances. I wasn't all that attractive, and in telling these stories I don't mean to imply that I was. Rather, I want to emphasize the point that even in situations where you are a good employee and you are doing the best job you know how to do, you may still be faced with unfair circumstances, sometimes because of someone else's wrong behaviors.

I stayed at the next insurance agency for several years. I was grateful to have the opportunity to be the first female sales agent in what was at that time a male-dominated business. Thankfully one of the partners saw potential in me, sent me for personality testing, and then provided training in the areas where the tests revealed my aptitudes. Two years after I'd been there, I became pregnant and had a very difficult pregnancy. While I was hospitalized, the company replaced me. Firing people while they're on medical leave is illegal in most instances now, but unfair things continue to happen in the workplace all the time.

I found temporary work during the rest of the pregnancy – no one wanted to take a chance on hiring a pregnant woman who may or may not return after giving birth. Despite the rough pregnancy, when my baby was born, she was fine. When I held my daughter for the first time, I had the feeling of having family for the very first time in my life. Here was a human who was truly connected to me, who would want to be with me. I was grateful that my baby was fine; but within a short time, I learned that my marriage was not. I was shocked when I found out that throughout my pregnancy, my husband had been acting like he was single. I moved out, filed for divorce, and was alone again – this time with a little girl to raise.

Having no money and no one to turn to for help, I needed a job fast. I knew I didn't want to experience any of the craziness I'd seen in those smaller insurance agencies, so I looked in the yellow pages and found the agency that claimed to be the oldest and largest independent insurance agency in the area. The listing gave the name of the founder and chief executive officer, so I called him. The secretary screening his calls asked who I was and why I was calling. She sounded as though she had no intention of putting my call through, but I asked that she let him know that I was on the line and had something he needed. Not knowing what to make of me, she put me on hold. The next thing I heard was the deep, gruff voice of an old man.

The agency owner identified himself and asked me how I had obtained his name. He asked what I wanted, and I told him that I didn't "want" anything but that I could do something for him! I told him that I was so confident in my ability to do my job that I would work for him for free for six months. If I had not met my goals at the end of that time, I would quietly leave. On the other hand, if I had met my goals, I would ask that he pay me a stipulated amount. He laughed and asked when he could meet me.

I was prepared for the question, dressed and ready to go, and told him I could be at his office in twenty minutes. He hired me on the spot and, of course, paid me from the first day. That man took me under his wing, taught me, and encouraged me. I worked there for nearly seven years and gained an education about insurance sales and service that had been unavailable anywhere else.

After my mentor retired, the remaining owners teased me with talk of ownership. I wanted more than to be an employee at someone else's mercy for the rest of my life; I wanted greater control of my destiny. If I owned my own company and did well in my work, I'd be rewarded financially; if I screwed up, I'd pay the price. But there would no longer be someone who "collected" my prizes in sales contests or who decided arbitrarily what, if anything, to pay me for salary, commissions, or bonuses. To me, an arbitrary bonus felt like giving a dog a bone. If you sat up and begged or stood on your hind legs and turned around three times, you got the treat. If not, you left hungry. When they made the decision to restructure my department, which would have decreased my income significantly, I felt demoralized and unvalued. All of the financial goals that I had set for myself were set back by what felt like an eternity.

The company owners never did offer me ownership, and they declined my proposal to start a new division of their agency dedicated to protecting homes for abused children. So, on May 2, 1989, after recovering from surgery to remove cancer, I did what seemed to everyone who knew me to be the least sensible thing anyone could do. I gave my notice and quit my job – the one that provided the stable income, health insurance, and life insurance.

With the encouragement and support of my dear friend and mentor, Corky Kindsvater, who was then the CEO of Hillview Acres Children's Home, I started my own insurance agency, insuring only homes for abused children. I've worked to protect child welfare agencies throughout the United States since then. I'm proud that through the years my companies, Human Services Insurance and Child Welfare Insurance Services, have done a tremendous amount of good for people and organizations that care for hurting children and families. Now, Markel Insurance Company, the company that bought Child Welfare Insurance, is carrying on and expanding the work of protecting people and organizations that care for children and families.

Looking back at all the experiences that led to my present life, there are so many people I am grateful for knowing. I wouldn't own my own insurance agency now if it hadn't been for my first boss, Chuck Wheeler, a Farmers Insurance Agent who took a chance and gave a job to a 15-year-old. I'm grateful that he answered all my questions, took the time to give me reading material that helped me begin to understand the business of insurance, and allowed me to try to do everything an unlicensed person could do. When my application for a test date for an insurance license was denied because I was under age 18, Chuck encouraged me to appeal to the Department of Insurance to be allowed to sit for my agent's license exam.

At Chuck's suggestion, I wrote to the Insurance Commissioner requesting that he take into consideration that I was an emancipated minor and that he allow me to take the test as any other adult. After several appeals, the Commissioner granted my request. I remember leaving the Los Angeles office of the Department of Insurance after having passed that test. I looked at my watch; it was not quite 10:00 a.m. I stood there on the street looking at the sights I'd never seen before, knowing that something big had just happened. I was changed. Everything had changed. I had navigated the traffic and driven myself into Los Angeles for the first time. Amazingly, I had found the right address. With knots in my stomach, I finally found a place to park. I was in awe of the big buildings and the hectic cars and people who rushed passed. I knew that because I had spent weeks studying the California Insurance Code book, had gotten myself out of my warm bed at 5:00 a.m., and did something I was scared to death to do, I had accomplished something that was going to change my life. I was the youngest licensed insurance agent in the state of California.

I'm grateful that Fred Livermore gave an opportunity to a brash 21-year-old kid and provided the experience and education I needed to become the insurance professional I am today. More importantly, I'm thankful to him for introducing me to the co-worker who became my sister-in-law, to the client who is and has been one of my dearest friends for over twenty years, and to the client who is now my husband. That job was very, very good for me!

Had I not made the phone call to Fred Livermore right when I did, and had I been timid during that phone call or during that first meeting, and had I not been dressed and ready to rush right over to his office to meet him, I never would have obtained the job that led to the family, the friends, and the business I have now. That job led to insuring that first home for abused children, which led to making a commitment to insure only homes for abused children, which has been a source of fulfillment in my life since 1989.

I'm grateful for Corky Kindsvater and his wife, Gayle, for entrusting the protection of Hillview Acres Children's Home to me and for encouraging me to "throw myself with reckless abandon" into protecting people and organizations who care for hurting, vulnerable children.

I've only told you a fraction of what I've experienced, but hopefully now you know that I never received anything for free. Rather, I've suffered some very unfair circumstances, and I've worked hard for everything I have.

The details of the dysfunction and abuse I experienced may be dramatically different from what you experienced, but it doesn't matter. What matters is that you know that everyone, whether he or she appeared to come from a "good home" or has been a child prostitute on the streets, has felt real pain.

The key to doing something significant with your life is in learning everything you can from what you've experienced, from the people who have influenced you *for good or bad*, and from the well-meaning people who have tried to help you and to teach you. The education and experience that you've gained from all of these people are clues to your purpose, to your life assignment.

You are responsible for your thoughts, words, and actions.

If the advice in this book is going to make a difference in your life, it's important that you understand that although I don't know exactly what you have gone through, I do know what it is to be under the control of someone else. I know what it feels like to suffer. I know about the personality quirks that result from childhood abuse. I know what it is like to have the vague feeling that something is wrong with you. I know what it feels like to be depressed, hopeless, and physically used up.

Regardless of whether you came from a loving family, experienced horrific abuse, or anything in between, you are responsible for your thoughts, your words, and your actions today and every day hereafter for the rest of your life. Although you may have wonderful friends and family in your life who care deeply about you, the truth is that no one wants to hear you go on and on about what happened to you years ago. They likely don't want to hear great details about what happened yesterday! Everyone has his or her own life, concerns, and story.

The very first step to the five points of prosperity, health, joy, peace, good relationships, and financial stability, is to take responsibility, effective immediately, for the quality of your life. You may say, *"Right. How do I do that?"* Well, you start by considering what good has come from the people and the experiences in your life. For the purposes of "mining the lessons" out of the experiences of your life, stop blaming people for what they have done to you or failed to do for you.

Stick with me, and I'll give you specific things you can do that are proven to result in true and complete prosperity.

CHAPTER 4

WHY WE DO WHAT WE DO

F irst let me assure you that however bad your circumstances are right at this moment, *it won't always be like this*. By reading this now and by doing your best to implement the suggestions here, you are doing exactly what is necessary to change everything in your life. But before I give you specific things you can do to begin to feel better immediately, let's talk about the impact of our past hurts on our actions.

Believing that *we are deserving* of good doesn't come easily to someone who was hurt at a very young and vulnerable age. We develop our first bit of self-worth and make our very first decision about whether we're good or bad, deserving or unworthy, precious or unwanted from the reflection in the eyes of those who are supposed to care for us. When we're young, we have no ability to put another person's anger, hurt, disappointment, pressures, etc., into perspective. So, if our caregiver looks at us with anger or frustration, speaks in an angry tone of voice, or handles us roughly, we intrinsically believe (on a very primitive, non-verbal level) that we are the cause, source, and focus of that anger.

Conversely, if a child sees happiness and fulfillment in his mother's eyes, hears a calm, loving voice, and is touched gently and lovingly, he thinks he's the cause, source, and focus of that happiness. That is the root of solid self-esteem. For those of us who didn't have someone under whose care we found our worth, it is up to us to intentionally make the change in our hearts and minds and DECIDE that we are deserving of good things – that we are worthy, loveable, and even precious.

Everyone wants love, approval, and respect; we want to be cared for and cared about. We want to feel that others think we're valuable and lovable. But many of us who were hurt at an early age fear being unloved and unwanted, stemming from wounds resulting from situations we cannot even recall – from things that happened before we were able to talk.

For example, a baby left in the crib for a day or two soaked in urine and feces, hungry, cold, scared, and in pain from an aching stomach and painful rashes may later, as an adult, feel a vague fear of being left alone without ever even being able to describe it verbally to anyone. A baby who gets no response at all to his or her cries eventually quits crying. This baby grows into a person who doesn't bother complaining or voicing his or her concerns because "it does no good anyway."

Little children who are hit unexpectedly, screamed at, told ugly things, kept confined, humiliated, violated, isolated, ridiculed, criticized, or left behind (while other children are allowed to do things) can experience residual effects that they may not even be fully aware of or may not be able to explain.

Many of us tend to think we're responsible for **everything**. If someone is grouchy, we start looking around for what we can do or say that will "fix" the situation and make it better. If someone is in a bad mood, we wonder if he or she is mad at us. Was there something

I did wrong? Something I said? Something I forgot to do?

Others of us do just the opposite and blame everyone else for everything that goes wrong, failing to take responsibility for anything. Either way, damaged people automatically make everything about *themselves* and jump to conclusions.

If someone doesn't return a phone call right away, fails to send a birthday card, or never does get around to setting up a promised lunch date, some of us automatically think something is wrong with us. Others of us assume the one who let us down meant to hurt us or is a jerk. Often, the truth is that the other person is simply involved in his or her own life, not thinking about us at all!

People who are extremely sensitive are very difficult to have as friends because there is a constant sense that you have to choose your words carefully to avoid hurting them. That's just too much work for most people to put into a friendship. If having quality relationships is important to you, and it should be, don't expect others to heal your hurts. Remind yourself that everyone has hurts and challenges. (*Later, I'll give you some specific suggestions on* **how** *to create and maintain good relationships.*)

When I was a little girl, even when I did do something well, it earned only a temporary good mood and a momentary absence of violence. As in many dysfunctional environments, the absence of violence did not equal peace. Even during those times of "cease fire," I was thinking of what had worked and what had failed to provide some momentary calm. I thought that if I could be good enough, perform well enough, work hard enough, or score high enough, I'd be rewarded with approval. The flaw in this logic common to victims of abuse is that there are no conditions that will result in approval because the person from whom we seek approval is damaged.

Unfortunately, it would never take long before something

happened to tip the delicate balance in my house the wrong way. My grandfather could move through the hairpin turn of moods at breakneck speed. He could plunge to the depths of depression faster than a descending bungee jumper. Consequently, I was on a never-ending roller coaster of trying to keep him in a good mood. It became my responsibility to try to keep him "fixed," an impossible job. Many of us from dysfunctional environments feel a tremendous pressure to perform. Often we feel responsible to keep everyone in our lives happy. Others of us shut down and find a way to escape.

I recall teachers and school counselors measuring my straight-A

Most of us from dysfunctional backgrounds immediately focus on what's wrong with us or flawed about us as a result of what's been done to us that we had absolutely no control over.

report cards against my ulcer and regularly appearing migraines and trying to get me to relax and be okay with passing grades rather than pressuring myself to get perfect grades. I understand why they said what they said, but I am hardwired with a desire to do well. So rather than fight it, I made it work for me. If you feel pressure, rather than using cigarettes, drugs, alcohol, sex, or any other ways to medicate or distract yourself, use that pressure to push you to improve your life.

History tells us that a lot of the people who have accomplished great things experienced serious adversity in their childhood. The people who give up or medicate themselves ultimately get nothing but more pain. But the people who harness the pressure they feel and accomplish great things do so in large part because they are driven to accomplish, to gain approval, and to earn their worthiness. In other words, as in my case and the cases of many people who overcame tremendous adversity, we did so not **despite** what we endured, but **because** of it.

Others make choices that result in incarceration. As crazy as it may sound, I suspect that two reasons for the high recidivism rate is the structure provided by prison life and the feeling of those incarcerated that they "belong" there. Inmates, like gangs, offer a sense of family in a distorted way. On some level, people who come from an unstable environment often gravitate toward structure. People from dysfunctional families like the structure and stability

Once I learned how to direct all the anger and tension that I felt into work, I found the desire for approval to be the primary motivating factor in my life.

of knowing there are rules that can be understood and mastered. We can work within them, keep score by them, and know when "we're okay." The military can be an excellent option for people who need to belong, who like structure, and who want to make a contribution to something bigger than themselves.

If you're angry, as I was for many years, rather than feeling guilty for the anger that you haven't yet let go of, channel that anger into your work. Yes, getting rid of it is the best thing. But it's a lot easier said than done. The best revenge for those of us who were the victims of unfair circumstances is to be wildly successful!

If people mistreated you, in essence what they did was take away your control when you were powerless to prevent it. But by carrying anger toward them as adults, we voluntarily enable them to continue to control us now. I refuse to give up one more minute of my life in anger or any other negative emotion for something that happened years ago that I cannot change. I encourage you to do the same. Eventually, you can get to a place where remembrances no longer sting.

People who grew up in dysfunctional environments draw some of these conclusions:

> No one can be trusted.
> The world is a scary place.
> If I don't expect anything good to happen, I won't be disappointed.
> It is only a matter of time until the next bad thing happens.
> I am worthless. No one wants me.

We draw these assumptions because our experiences with people have reinforced and validated them. Consider, though, that the "evidence" that formed our opinions came from damaged people and unhealthy relationships. Recognizing and accepting that these assumptions might not be correct after all is the most difficult part of changing our lives. And the only effective way to truly change these assumptions is not by someone TELLING us that we should change, that our opinions are wrong, that things will get better, or any of the other things that well-meaning people say. *The way to change what we believe is for us to have experiences and relationships that support new beliefs.* This starts with stepping back and objectively considering all the things we believe, and then questioning those beliefs. When we're open to considering that perhaps our assumptions are flawed, we become open to change, open to other people, and open to the new experiences and relationships that will support a foundation of new, more accurate beliefs.

Here's an example: When I was in my twenties, as ridiculous as it sounds, I realized I didn't like redheads. It wasn't that I didn't like the hair color; it was a feeling of vague discomfort every time I was around an adult with red hair. I didn't know why and couldn't explain it. Then one day the light went on in my head! I remembered that when I was very young, a lady with bright red hair took me to the ocean to teach me to swim. I was knocked over by a wave, swallowed water, and had sand in my eyes, ears, mouth, and everywhere else I could have sand. I was terrified. I remember looking around trying to get my bearings and seeing this lady and her friend sitting on a blanket on the sand looking at me and laughing. I was frightened of her and somehow associated her red hair with what I perceived as meanness. Once I understood the connection between that experience and red hair, I was able to intentionally "undo" that completely unrelated connection.

The truth is that there is no place where we can ever live, no job at which we can ever work, and no relationship that we can ever be in where everything is going to be perfect.

We are survivors. We are strong. We are complete and okay by ourselves. In other words, if you are trying to find that one person who's going to make it all right, forget it. The giant job of making you okay is simply too much pressure to put on any other person. No one can live up to your expectations and meet all your needs. Sometimes we push people away and are mean to others just to see if they'll stick around. Sometimes we shut people out to keep from getting hurt. Sometimes we're overly nice, generous to a fault, and even overextend ourselves in order to get people to like us.

I finally was able to truly get rid of all of the anger that I felt toward those who had hurt me, but it took a long time. I'll tell you how I did it later. But in the meantime, if you're angry or feeling bad about the unfairness you've experienced, give yourself a break. You don't have to feel guilty for feeling anger that is a natural response to unwarranted, unfair things that have happened to you.

The truth is that there is no place where we can ever live, no job at which we can ever work, and no relationship that we can ever be in where everything is going to be perfect. Even really good people will let you down every now and then. And although there are some truly good people in the world, there seems to be an endless supply of knuckleheads, jokers, and jackasses who are our neighbors, co-workers, bosses, friends, and family. The good news is that the skills we learned for coping with the challenges we faced as vulnerable children equip us to handle everything we face as adults. In fact, we can handle things that would destroy some people.

STRAIGHTENING OUT THE "CROOKED" PLACES

When young children are mistreated or abused, their personalities get wounded. Those wounds heal, but sometimes they heal with a lot of painful scar tissue. Sometimes, like a broken bone set incorrectly or not set at all, we heal "crooked," meaning that our personality is somehow distorted. In places where we have "healed crooked," we tend to be overly sensitive, to get angry, and to react in ways that don't make sense to people around us. These inappropriate responses to the situations of life are what ruin potentially good relationships. I want to help you identify those "crooked places" and help you straighten them out so that you won't hurt there anymore, and you won't damage good relationships.

I realized somewhere between the ages of 35 and 45 that I no longer needed the skills of manipulation that had protected me as a child. Yet, undoing something that was knitted so tightly into the fibers that made up my personality took much work to undo.

You can be hurt to the same degree that you allow others to get close enough to love you. So, through isolation and intimidation, I had erected a wall to protect myself so that no one ever hurt me again. What I didn't understand was that in doing so, I made sure no one could get close enough to love me.

Treating people right and making right choices gets easier as you mature. Maturity precedes complete healing. Healing is necessary for true happiness.

What it took me years to learn was that you always get hurt by the poison you give to other people. Of course, I'm not talking about literally giving someone poison. I'm talking about saying unkind things about someone (*even when you're telling something that is true*), lying to people, raising your voice to someone, doing physical harm to another person, saying harmful words, and taking any other wrong action. Although it may not make sense to you now, trust me when I tell you that your wrong actions or words WILL ultimately hurt you more than they'll hurt the other person.

In my work of protecting homes for abused children, I find myself dealing with tragedies involving children in foster care. These situations are highly emotionally charged, so even with all the progress I've made in forgiving people who've hurt me, letting go of the anger I carried for so many years, and just learning how to be a decent person, there are still times when I'll read a report of a foster care tragedy or someone will say or do something that touches too close to an old heartache, which triggers a hurt, impatient, irritated, or downright rude response from me.

"Normal people" don't understand how others who have experienced extreme adversity can be fine one minute and angry or withdrawn the next. They don't understand that the change in attitude or mood can be triggered by something as seemingly insignificant as a song on the radio, the mention of a name, or the sight of something or someone that is a reminder of the source of pain. For example, for a rape victim, a song that was playing during the rape will forever be a reminder of that awful event. Or the name of an abuser, or anything that reminds the victim of that person, can instantly trigger a flood of ugly emotion.

I would like to say that I've come so far that now I'm always in a good mood and never angry, hurt, or frustrated, but that simply would not be true. I'm infinitely better than I used to be, but I still occasionally feel negative emotions. The difference is the change in my actions. Instead of lashing out at the unfortunate people who happen to cross my path, now when I get irritable I keep my distance as much as possible. To avoid saying or doing anything that might hurt anyone, I warn those around me that I'm not in a good mood and apologize if I say anything that could be construed as hurtful. During those times, it might be a bit longer than usual for people to get a return phone call from me. People who know me know I'm not trying to be rude – I'm going out of my way NOT to take a chance of being snappy or rude.

People closest to me, who have no choice but to interact with me regardless of my mood or circumstances, either get to a place where they don't easily take offense or they put a little more distance between us during those times. Having said all this, the good news is that we're not alone in having quirks in our personalities. Everyone has them, although some of us more than others. All of us are the result of our experiences, our choices, our failures, our actions and failures to act, and the words we've spoken or failed to speak. All of us have our sensitivities, emotions, moods, and attitudes.

WHAT DOES IT MEAN TO BE YOURSELF?

When I was a child, without even realizing what was happening, I became extremely sensitive to the slightest change in facial expression and tone of voice. There was nowhere to hide in the little shack we lived in, so out of necessity I learned that there were things I could do to avoid or mitigate trouble. I lived in a constant state of vigilance, believing that at any time I might have to defend myself. I also learned when it made more sense to just silently take what was being dealt.

After sixteen years, I became what others wanted me to be. I didn't know what my true personality was like. When my high school counselor sent me on a job interview, she told me, *"Just be yourself."* I had no idea what that meant or how to do that. Like others in dysfunctional environments, I rarely saw appropriate behavior modeled. I never saw conflict resolved other than by yelling, screaming, or hitting. In fact, "being me" meant working hard to please everyone around me to make sure that no one was angry or disappointed in me, that no one was violent, and that everything went along uneventfully.

People who were abused as children or who lived in dysfunctional environments often feel shame. Although I didn't understand it until long after I was out on my own, I realized much later that throughout my childhood I was ashamed of the abuse and wouldn't have considered telling anyone what was going on. The one time the police did show up at my house, my grandfather met the officer out in front of the house, chatted and laughed a bit as though they were old buddies, and smiled and waved as the officer drove away.

When my grandfather walked back into the house, he unleashed a fury worse than I had ever experienced.

I was ashamed of being left by my parents, so I lied to the kids and teachers at school, saying that my mom and dad couldn't wait until they could come back for me. I was ashamed of the house we lived in, so I lied about where I lived and why I couldn't have anyone over. I was ashamed of the fact that we didn't have enough money, so I lied about why I couldn't go to the movies, join Girl Scouts, or do any of the things the other kids did.

For many of us, being "ourselves" isn't a good feeling because of the undercurrent of shame or the sense of being unwanted or "damaged goods." But the truth is that we can heal, we are resilient, we are loveable, and we don't need to be rescued – we can rescue ourselves!

Whether it was through abuse of some kind, divorce, sickness, or some other unfortunate circumstances, many of us are living unhappy lives. The good news is that you are reading this now, and you are no longer unable to defend yourself, no longer completely vulnerable, no longer weak, and no longer powerless. **You can** overcome whomever or whatever adversely affected you. But before that can happen, you must figure out who you are and decide who you want to be. You must make a decision to exercise your power to find and fulfill your purpose. Regardless of what has happened to you or what your life is like right now, you can learn how to intentionally create the person you want to become. I'll tell you how to find your purpose and create the "new you" a little later.

YOUR PAST: DEAL WITH IT — THEN FORGET IT!

Many people have lived through unspeakable abuse, the horrors of wartime combat, or a traumatic event such as rape or some other violent crime. Some choose to leave their story untold all of their lives. The last thing they want to do is relive the trauma by talking about it. In addition to much of the past being just too painful to tell, there are other reasons many choose to keep silent about abuse suffered.

For some, our abusers convinced us at an impressionable age that no one would believe us and we would just be humiliated and/or laughed at if we told what happened. Others keep quiet because of pressure from family members to keep the peace. *Talk about adding insult to injury.* Some of us have buried our pain so deeply that we've convinced ourselves that nothing ever happened – that maybe it was just a nightmare. Others go along with the family's rewritten history, putting on a performance of pretending that whatever painful events we heard, saw, or experienced never happened or weren't nearly as bad as remembered. Or we have arrived, at long last, at a relationship everyone involved can live with, and we know

You cannot be successful in life while thinking and talking about how unfair your life has been.

that dredging up the past would ruin the delicate balance we've created. Still others have a new life with people who don't know the ugly truth, and we fear that if the truth came out, the people we care about would think less of us or the relationship would be ruined.

Many of us who have been mistreated are reluctant to make ourselves vulnerable to others. We are vulnerable to the people who mistreated us, to others who for whatever reason failed to protect us, and anyone else with whom we share our story. When we tell the details of what happened to us and how we felt about it, we're unprotected against the next time someone inadvertently or, God forbid, intentionally picks the emotional scab off.

For this reason, many of us intentionally distance ourselves from anyone who was involved or who knows our story. We give only a glimpse into our painful past and steer clear of anything that would bring it to our remembrance.

Others of us choose to have whatever quality of relationship we can have with our abusers because we tend to think that even a weak, unstable, or phony connection to some family is better than having absolutely no one. Some feel a sense of obligation to an ailing or frail former abuser. These people have either fully forgiven everyone involved or they have buried the pain so deep that they're able to put on Academy Award quality performances for best supporting role in a family where even the "family" is as much of a façade as a Hollywood movie set.

Many of us go through life never fully healing and never fully understanding why the mistreatment happened. Though logic tells us that as young children we couldn't have deserved the abuse, we tend to discount the logic in favor of the old reruns that play in our heads when we find ourselves alone on special days, feel physical pain, or have any other experience that reminds us of what we experienced when we were powerless to prevent it. In fact, it typically doesn't take much for some of us to "flash back" to a time when we felt unloved, abandoned, rejected, or worthless.

It's interesting that so many people think that they've dealt with the past, they really don't have a problem, and everything is fine so there is no reason to dredge anything up. That may be true, but before you assume that you don't need to deal with your past, consider that we each have a specific limit on our ability to be patient, kind, gentle (or fill in here any other positive character trait). Our ability to treat others "right" all really stems from feeling loved. Those of us who were loved as children and/or feel loved and accepted as adults typically have a greater "emotional bank account" of love, which shows up in our ability to behave patiently and with kindness toward people and situations that would frustrate us. In other words, when we feel loved and wanted, it takes longer for someone to push us to the point of anger.

To the degree that we do not feel loved and accepted, our "emotional bank account" is depleted, so there is not enough patience, kindness, gentleness, etc., to give out when we need it to keep peace and resolve conflict. When there's not much in the

---

When we feel loved and wanted, it takes longer for someone to push us to the point of anger.

"account," it doesn't take much to set us off. For example, most people behave properly until they experience some major pain, such as being betrayed by a loved one or fired from a job. On the other hand, those of us who feel unloved and unwanted often barely control our anger when someone cuts us off in traffic.

It's important to deal with your past and then forget it because until we do, we are unable to accept love from others. When we think about our past, we remind ourselves of being unlovable and unwanted. When we feel that way, our "emotional bank account" runs low. When our "account" is low, we damage our relationships by acting inappropriately. For example, although we may look like well-adjusted people, when we feel unloved, we are more likely to yell, use foul language, or get physical for reasons that make no sense to the people around us. When we lose our temper over someone cutting in front of us in line or moving into our lane on the freeway, it takes people by surprise. No one wants to be around someone who is unpredictable, volatile, or violent.

People whose reactions are disproportionate to the situation are like a chair that's been carefully balanced on only three legs. If one leg is completely missing, the chair can be propped up and balanced, but it doesn't take much to tip it over. Those of us who haven't dealt with our anger about whatever unfairness we've experienced are like that precariously balanced chair. It doesn't take much to offend us. (Think of it as "off-ending" or tipping over that chair.) We walk around a good deal of the time hurt, angry, depressed, or a combination of all three. The truth is that until we deal with the anger, like the chair that's missing a leg, we will not be able to do all we should be capable of doing.

So, if you're someone who thinks you've dealt effectively with the pain you've experienced, yet you are easily angered, often impatient, frequently depressed, or rarely feel emotion at all, consider that your brain may have figured out a way either to bury the pain or compartmentalize it. In the worst scenarios, the human mind can create different personalities to shift in and out of in order to hide from the pain. The good news is that there are ways that really work to release the anger. Once you figure out what works for you, you'll feel better, you'll be able to "*make deposits into your emotional bank account,*" and you'll be better able to love and be loved by others.

People who don't deal with their past and forget it never receive all of the benefits that should accompany success. Some achieve financial success only to ask themselves if that's all there is. Many turn to drugs and alcohol to numb their physical and emotional pain.

Regardless of whether you are the type of person who has never told anyone what you've been through, you've told everyone who would listen, or you are somewhere in between, it's important that you do not continue to bring up the past. If you feel that you have effectively dealt with your past, then quit thinking about it and talking about it. If you haven't entirely dealt with your past, in the next chapter, I'll give you some specific things you can do immediately that will help you get to the point that you can truly move on.

DON'T REPEAT THE PAST

Unfortunately, some of us grow up to perpetuate the abuse or dysfunction by mistreating the people closest to us. This is particularly heartbreaking when someone who was abused becomes an abuser. Sadly, it happens all too frequently. Surely no one ever intends to abuse his or her children, but if we don't "unlearn the wrong" and intentionally learn appropriate parenting or see it modeled for us, we are likely to repeat the only parenting behavior with which we are familiar. I was one of those.

Although I knew I never wanted to hurt my child, and I went to great lengths not to hit her, the anger and frustration that was always right under the surface bubbled up with little provocation. And although I had desperately sought approval as a child, I suppose because I had never received it or saw it modeled, I didn't know how to give it to my daughter. If she got all A's and a B, I focused on the B. I criticized her and pressured her to do better, regardless of how well she'd done. I never showed any appreciation for all the wonderful characteristics of her personality or applauded her efforts. In some distorted, "crooked" way, I thought that if I congratulated her for what she'd done well, she'd slack off on the areas that needed work.

What I didn't realize was that I was trying to mold my daughter into the person I had been – driven and ambitious, wanting to fix everything and everyone, and with an unwavering focus on financial success. (*Back then I thought that money would "fix" everything.*) Our personalities were different. But instead of loving the beautiful person she was and celebrating our differences, I focused only on what I thought was my responsibility: to "improve her," just like my grandfather, in his warped way, always tried to improve me.

As a mother I did and said a lot of things that I shouldn't have, and I failed to do and say a lot that a good mother should. As a result, I was the cause of a lot of pain for my precious girl. Now, my daughter and I have a wonderful relationship. I've apologized for everything in general and every detail I can remember. I've done all I know how to do to make up for the time when I wasn't a very good parent. We've both benefited from counseling, and she knows that I did the best I could with what I knew at the time, and that I've always loved her.

If you've made mistakes with people in your life, it's never too late to say you're sorry. As long as everyone involved is still breathing, it's not too late to change. Regardless of how the person responds to the change in you or to your apology, take the step. This one thing will help you avoid repeating the past.

You may not have had any control over what has happened in your life, but you do have control from this point forward. Regardless of what you've done or what you've experienced, make a decision today **not** to repeat the past.

EVERYONE HAS FELT REJECTION

Rejection is a terrible feeling. It is a feeling of being unloved, not accepted, not good enough, unwanted, and unworthy.

Consider the feeling of being unimportant, of feeling that everyone is better than you. Have you ever felt the sinking feeling of walking into a room knowing that you're not dressed right or that you weren't invited, or that you just don't belong? It's because of feelings like this that you may do things you know you shouldn't do; for example, exaggerating your resume to make people like you and hire you, using drugs others are using to avoid looking like you don't fit in, or choosing NOT to pick up the phone to ask someone out for fear of rejection.

Before I understood that I could *choose* to think and feel differently, I felt that people were rejecting me when they disagreed with me, but they were merely rejecting my opinion or idea. Consequently, I tried to convince and persuade and manipulate people into agreement with me because I hated the feeling of rejection that accompanied disagreement.

When you experience rejection or exclusion by others, understand that you're not the only one who has had this feeling. Understand also that it won't be the last time. Even people born into loving families have experienced the pain of rejection, abandonment, or exclusion. It's a common human feeling. It's awful, but note what I said: IT'S A FEELING. While feelings can hurt to the bone, they're still just feelings, and you can change the way you feel by changing the way you think. More on this to come.

FOCUS ON OTHERS, NOT YOURSELF

Before you can take charge and begin to do the things that will literally change your life, you have to know the hard truth. What I'm about to tell you may sound really harsh. You might even think it sounds nuts. But if you will think about it, once you work through pain, disappointment, and self-pity, you'll see that I'm right.

Grief, anger and depression all stem from focusing on yourself and your problems. As long as we're focused on ourselves, on our pain, and on the unfairness in our lives rather than the needs of others, we'll remain angry, hurt, and depressed.

Getting the focus off ME needs to be a conscious effort that we may have to make for the rest of our lives. But it's worth it! When we're focused on us – *who's hurting us, who's saying something about us behind our backs, who took our parking space, who got the promotion we deserved, who broke up with us, who didn't invite us to their party, etc., etc.* – we feel pain, anger, self-pity, frustration, hopelessness, and other negative emotions.

On the other hand, when we choose to focus on other people, trying to understand what's wrong with them and why they are behaving the way they do, we feel better. When we know what's going on in their lives or who has hurt them so badly that they say unkind things, act like jerks, or forget about commitments they've made, it's easier to overlook and forgive their words and actions. When we focus on trying to understand and help others rather than

> *You're likely to make similar mistakes because of the selfishness of holding on to anger, bitterness, and resentment.*

focusing on our own feelings, we overcome our negative emotions. We're not stopped in our tracks from moving toward our goals because of the pain inflicted by another, so we accomplish more.

Once you've begun to consider other people's feelings and circumstances, take this one step farther. To really get your mind off your problems, alleviate depression, create and improve your relationships, and create opportunities to improve your own life, you must look for ways to help others. *This is no typo!* I did not say, *"Help yourself."* I said, *"Look for ways to help others!"* The reason for this is simple: If you are thinking about someone else, you are not focused on your problems. And in the midst of helping someone else, you will often make friends and find solutions to problems that previously appeared insurmountable.

You may be saying, *"Lady, you don't know what I've been through or my circumstances now. If you did, you'd know I have to focus on the problems facing me right now."* Or, you may be saying, *"I'll try it, but I don't even know where to start."* You can begin immediately with the people closest to you – your family, your neighbors, your co-workers, and your acquaintances. If you want to meet new people, consider joining a club that does something of interest to you or a group of people who are in similar situations as you are. Or consider volunteering at a local homeless shelter, a food bank, a church, or some other organization that does good work.

Regardless of your current circumstances, if you approach people with an attitude of *"what can I do to help you?"* you'll be amazed at the things that work out and the changes that take place.

CHAPTER 5

GET OVER THE HURT AND AVOID BEING HURT AGAIN

I f you easily recall the painful events of your past or the hurtful words of others, there are steps you can take to stop the hurt and prevent future pain. Here are *proven ways to stop the past from hurting you* that cost nothing more than a little of your time.

Change the channel in your mind. Learning to control your thoughts is so important that I've devoted an entire section to it later in the book. In the meantime, begin to consider that you have the power to change what you think about the same way that you have the power to change the channel on a television. Once you master this technique, you'll no longer be a victim of hurtful memories. Rather, you'll be in control of those memories.

Completely forgive the person or people who hurt you. This means really letting the pain go and expecting nothing in return from the person, not even an apology. In fact, expecting the person to give you something to "make up for" what he or she has done to you really isn't forgiveness. That's like "selling" your forgiveness in exchange for the gift. This is a proven technique for taking control of your life. I say this because it's truly the only thing that will completely release YOU. Trying to hold accountable people who hurt you is natural. *They deserve to be punished. They deserve to have done to them what they did to you. They do not deserve forgiveness. They don't deserve pity. They don't deserve a "pass" for their behavior because of whatever adversity they've experienced.* They may not deserve you giving them the time of day. But remember that forgiveness isn't for them. It's for YOU. This requires a high degree of maturity, so if you are not ready, come back to this one. But DO come back to this at some point in your life.

If you fail to forgive others who have hurt you, the bitterness and resentment that inevitably comes from unforgiveness will absolutely, unequivocally, undoubtedly keep you from achieving and enjoying everything that you are capable of having and doing.

> *Forgiveness isn't for them.*
> *It's for YOU.*

Change your emotions about a memory by changing the memory. I realize this may sound ridiculous, but it can be very effective in taking the sting out of the memory. How do you change something that's already happened? First, intentionally recall a painful event. Then imagine the event happening differently. For example, imagine that a big, strong person walks in and stops the other person from inflicting pain on you, or that you are able to get away or disable the person before he or she is able to hurt you. If the situation involves hurtful words, imagine yourself saying just the right thing that stops the person in his or her tracks or someone else walking in and saying the thing that makes the person stop. In doing this, you are literally rewriting your history so that it no longer has the power to hurt you.

Write the details of a painful event. If you do this on a computer, after you've written all of the details, highlight the whole thing and hit the delete key. Literally wipe the whole thing off of your computer screen and out of your memory. If you write about the painful event on paper, when you are through, tear it into tiny pieces and flush it down the toilet. This symbolizes that you are taking control of your life and getting rid of the whole event.

Determine not to give anyone who's hurt you one more minute of your life. Hit the "delete" key on bad memories.

Avoid putting yourself in situations that would allow an abuser to hurt you again. Although this advice may sound simple and self-explanatory, it can be more complicated than it appears. For example, if an employee is being taken advantage of by someone in authority at work, it would be irresponsible to just quit the job without finding another one first. In a case such as this, the person must evaluate his or her circumstances to determine what can be done immediately to stop the abuse, such as asking for a transfer, avoiding situations where the person is alone with the abuser, telling someone else in authority about the situation, and looking for another job.

As another example, some people feel obligated to attend family functions and events or to go other places where their abuser is expected to show up. The pressure of obligation and the anxiety of the anticipation of seeing someone who has hurt us can wreak havoc in our lives. This is doubly difficult if no one other than the abuser is aware of what's happened. When this is the case, the person who doesn't attend or the person who chooses to attend but then acts angry or cold toward the abuser while there may be seen by others as the one in the wrong. Regardless of the situation and the concern about who might judge you, I encourage you to decide not to put yourself in situations where you can be hurt again by someone who has a history of hurting you. Give yourself permission to avoid seeing these people and going to places that could result in more hurt.

Learn what works for you when people upset you or mistreat you. For example, find a place where you can be alone to collect your thoughts and decide your best action – lock yourself in the bathroom if that's the only place you can be alone. Other immediate actions you can try are to take a deep breath before you respond, walk away, go work out, or take some other healthy action that will get your mind off of the situation to allow you time to cool down before you respond. DON'T medicate yourself with nicotine, alcohol, or some kind of drug to get your mind off your emotions.

Identify the characteristics of people who are likely to hurt you in the future, and be careful about being in relationships with them. How can you spot people who are likely to hurt you? People who have been hurt are more likely to hurt you than someone who feels loved. How do you recognize people who've been hurt? Here are some characteristics:

- They are unpleasant to be around.
- They use their past or their pain as an excuse for bad behavior.
- They frequently talk about themselves and their issues.
- They are jealous of other people or what they have, and jealousy is a sign of insecurity.

- They get angry easily and frequently.

- They are often depressed.

- They are vulgar.

- They are immature and act childishly.

- They act pitifully so that people will know they are hurting in the hopes that people will ask about their feelings, giving them an opportunity to talk about their problems.

If you find someone frequently hoping for sympathy, remember, acting sad may get some sympathy, but that's all it will get anyone. It won't move anyone toward his or her goals or financial success. The ONLY thing that will move us toward achievement of all of our goals is genuine forgiveness.

Refuse to get hurt! Yes, I know that sounds ridiculous. But consider that you can choose to ignore a hurtful remark. You can choose to make a joke out of it. You can even pretend it wasn't said! You can choose to tell the person that what he or she said or did has hurt you and that you won't allow it to happen again. If it happens another time, you can choose not to be in a relationship with that person or just not spend much time with that person. Do not confide anything to hurtful people that would give them an opportunity to hurt you in the future.

In some cases, people are just trying to get a reaction out of you. So, reacting in anger plays right into their hands. When you refuse to react to a hurtful remark or action, the offending person often doesn't know what to do. If it happens on the job, and you must let your boss know about the incident or defend yourself to a boss or supervisor, do it without anger. The fact that you're composed and unhurt shows both your maturity and the idiocy of the other person. In personal or professional relationships, the best results come from being the best person you can be, treating everyone well

– including the one who hurt you – and waiting for the person who hurt you to be exposed for the fool he or she is.

Regarding making the conscious choice not to allow unkind words or actions to hurt you, consider that the Greek word for *offense*, as in taking offense when wronged, is *bait*. So in the Greek language, *to take offense* means literally to "take the bait," like a mouse getting caught in a trap while trying to take the cheese or a fish getting hooked while trying to take the bait off the hook. This is an excellent way of looking at getting offended or hurt. When we take offense to something someone says or does or fails to do, we are taking the bait and getting hurt or angry. Those emotions typically won't hurt the person who's offending us. Instead, they hurt us! Taking offense to a wrong done to us doesn't mean the person didn't

Determine not to give anyone the satisfaction of putting you in a bad mood or in a negative frame of mind.

do something wrong. Even if he or she <u>intended</u> to hurt us, we're still in control of whether or not we allow it to hurt us.

You may be saying, *"Right, how am I going to avoid being hurt when someone intentionally says something terrible to me?"* You are human, and you probably can't avoid feeling hurt initially. What I'm suggesting is that you **develop the ability** by practicing to dismiss or ignore the hurtful words or actions. If you fail to develop this ability, the one who is going to suffer from the hurt is **you.**

If you "take the bait," not only does it damage the relationship, but you lose your peace, you become less effective on your job and in your other relationships, and the one who tried to hurt you has SUCCEEDED IN DOING SO! Determine not to give anyone the satisfaction of putting you in a bad mood or in a negative frame of mind.

There are wrong ways to avoid being hurt:

- Hurt the other person first.

- Never let anyone close enough to hurt us.

- Be the first to leave.

- Pretend we're not really hurt. *(This can invite more mistreatment.)*

- Never trust anyone again.

The problem with all these actions is that they do not allow development of a committed relationship that ultimately results in the honest, unconditional love that will heal your hurts. Only unconditional love will bring the healing you need to be truly successful in every sense of the word. (When I say "successful," I'm talking about total prosperity where nothing in your life is missing and nothing is broken. It's feeling good both physically and emotionally, having great relationships, having enough money to do whatever you want to do and have whatever you want to have, and being free of fear.)

The consequences of not learning how to deal appropriately with hurt feelings and refusing to forgive those who hurt you are invisible and silent. You may not see them coming, but these negative actions start on the inside and move into every area of your life. The evidence of changes to your personality resulting from holding onto offense includes anger, skepticism, sarcasm, suspicion, and paranoia. If changes aren't made, this can lead to all kinds of physical problems that can steal the quality of your life.

You can train yourself to react properly to challenging situations. Just as you can train your body to exercise and build muscle, stamina, and strength, you can train your mind by practicing to hold back from saying something rude or hurtful. You can train yourself to smile when you'd rather scream, and train yourself to leave rather than doing something that will move you away from your goals instead of closer to them.

WHAT ARE YOU HOLDING ON TO?

If you choose not to try the suggested techniques or only give them a half-hearted attempt, what you are doing is choosing to hold on to the very thing that will prevent you from achieving your highest level of success. In choosing to hold on to negative thoughts, you are holding on to the pain, and ultimately you are giving the person who caused your pain control of your present and your future!

I held on to the pain of my abandonment and abuse for many, many years. No one faulted me for doing so. BUT, in doing that, I was giving even more of my life to the people who caused that pain so long ago. I determined that they had taken enough from me, and I was not going to give them one more minute of my life.

The times when I was wondering if my mother thought of me on my birthday or if she wondered what I looked like, or if my father ever wondered what I was doing or if I was okay, I was literally giving them that time and more. What do I mean by this? Well, every time I would hear my mother or father's name, or the names of the two kids my mother chose to keep, or anything else that reminded me of any of them, sadness would overtake me. I would walk around at work with tears in my eyes, withdraw from friends, lock myself in my room, and tell my little girl, "Mommy doesn't feel like playing right now." I'd usually wind up with a migraine or an upset stomach. In the meantime, the people responsible for my pain were living their lives, completely oblivious to whatever was going on in my life.

It would be a day or two before I was "normal" again. The time I should have been playing with my little girl and enjoying her was lost – forever. I can never get that back. I thought that by shutting myself off in my room I was avoiding an explosion of my temper that was always simmering just below the surface. I didn't want to take my problems out on my little girl.

Unfortunately, I hadn't yet learned how to avoid the hurt or what to do to get past feeling sad or angry, except to lock myself in my room or in the bathroom. Ironically, the fact that I was leaving my daughter alone to entertain herself was a form of abandonment that wasn't that far removed from the abandonment I'd experienced. I didn't understand that physically being in the same house, providing enough to eat, and not hitting her wasn't enough to qualify as a good parent. It wasn't until years later that I saw the effect of all this on her.

Had I just forgiven those people for leaving me and others for hurting me and failing to protect me, I could have avoided giving them any more of my time. The day or two that I would spend sulking after having been reminded of them was a day or two more I was giving them. Sadly, it was also a day or two of my young daughter's life that I was giving them. Well, those days are over. I've forgiven them all – truly let it all go. In fact, I feel sympathy for them.

If you will give these suggestions a chance, you will be taking the control away from the person responsible for your pain. But if you continue to allow past hurtful events to make you sad or angry, you will be hostage to those memories, and you will hold yourself back from doing what you are otherwise capable of doing.

Holding on to hurt will damage your current and future relationships because people don't want to be around those who are angry, bitter, and resentful. Yes, there are caring people who will help you through ugly emotions, but if you are someone who is "stuck," never actually getting over these feelings, eventually people will distance themselves from you. People don't choose angry, bitter, resentful people to be business partners, employees, or close friends. You will never know how many opportunities you miss out on if you choose not to let go of pain from the past.

FORGIVING IS ONE THING; FORGETTING IS SOMETHING ELSE!

You may be saying, *"But you don't know what they did to me!"* True. But it happened. It's over. You can't go back and change your past. But you can change your future. However, you never will if you don't forgive those who hurt you and stop thinking and talking about what happened. The people who hurt you may be hateful animals who don't deserve your forgiveness, or they may be just misguided individuals who had some pain in their lives that led them to make bad decisions. Regardless, CHOOSE to let it go and move on. If you choose not to forgive and fail to move on with your life, you may wind up no better than they were! You're likely to make similar mistakes because of the selfishness of holding on to anger, bitterness, and resentment.

> *Forgiveness, by definition,*
> *is undeserved.*

Yes, I said selfishness. We hold on to anger because we feel we're cheating ourselves if we let someone off for a wrong done to us. *"It isn't fair,"* we say. *"They haven't EARNED forgiveness."*

Rather than trying to get even with people who hurt you or

trying to prove that you've been treated unfairly, invest your time in improving your situation. If you don't quit thinking about the past, your future will include more pain. It may come from different people and circumstances, but more pain is guaranteed if you don't choose to stop thinking about past hurts.

Having said all this, I didn't say you had to be in relationship with someone who has hurt you. There is no need to put yourself in a position to be hurt again. I have forgiven my mother and my father and my grandparents and all the people who could have done something to help me but didn't. My grandparents have both passed away, but my mother and father may still be alive. Regardless, I am not seeking a relationship with them. Sometimes, just forgiving and moving on is the best you can do and the best thing for you. If you can't bear the thought of taking a chance on opening the door to more abuse, more rejection, repeated abandonment, people using you, or whatever hurt might await you, then don't even contact these people to let them know you've forgiven them. Just forgive them and move on.

Once you forgive those who caused you pain, "change the channel of your mind" so that you stop thinking about every hurtful thing ever said or done. Yes, I know it's easier said than done; but for your sake, do whatever you have to do to truly forgive so that your heart can begin to heal.

How do you forget?

First, you must make the conscious decision that you will not let your past pain hold you back from a good future. CHOOSE to smile and laugh, and try to find something amusing about every situation. Remember, walking around with a scowl or sad look on your face isn't going to get you anything but, perhaps, some pity. Being or looking pitiful will never move you toward success.

Second, ask yourself what good could come of every seemingly negative situation you face. Believe it or not, good can come from very difficult circumstances. Sometimes you have to search harder than others to find the positive, but doing so is well worth the effort because it changes your attitude.

Third, think about what you want in your future and then spend some time every day thinking about what it will be like when you have it. When you are thinking about your future, you cannot dwell on your past. Thinking of your future literally interrupts negative thoughts.

One way to help you think about and focus on your future rather than your past is to cut pictures out of magazines of the things you want to have, the places you want to go, the house you want to live in, the car you want to drive, etc. Visual images of the things you want are very powerful motivators. For years I kept a postcard of a Mercedes SL convertible pinned up in my cubicle at work.

At home I collected pictures of a beach house, beautiful places to vacation, and many other things I wanted. I glued them on a piece of poster board and looked at them first thing in the morning and last thing before I went to sleep. I looked at those pictures during the years that I lived in a dark, dingy apartment in a bad part of town, watched a little black and white television that only got three fuzzy stations, and drove cars I'd bought at the wrecking yard to fix up and sell. To look at my life during that time, it seemed absurd to think I'd ever have a house on the beach, a brand new Mercedes SL, and every other thing I wanted. But after years of learning how to forgive, figuring out how to avoid getting hurt again, working hard, and visualizing myself living the life I wanted, one by one, each of the things I had visualized became my reality.

PRACTICING WHAT I PREACH

I was the last person my grandfather saw before he died, the person who made sure he was properly taken care of, the person who combed his hair and washed his face for him the last day of his life. I was also the last person my grandmother ever saw. I was the one who moved her into my nice home from the dilapidated shack she lived in, made sure she had her medication and treatments on time, gave her whatever she wanted to eat, and made her last days comfortable. I was the one who held her as she took her last breath. Yes, the child they severely abused was the one who took care of them in their last days.

I'm sure my grandparents never expected that neither of their two children would be there for them when they needed someone most. They probably never considered that there would be a time when they would be the vulnerable, weak ones. Those two situations taught me that you just never know when the tables are going to turn. You don't know who is going to be with you or what your circumstances will be when you take your final breath. You never know when you are going to need someone to help you or just to be with you. So, take my advice and treat everyone in your life and everyone you meet with respect and kindness.

When I was 41, I decided for the first time ever to try to find my mother. Not to have a relationship with her or to expose myself to the disappointment, heartache, and complications that association could bring, but simply to let her know that I forgave her and that I have a great life. I wrote in a card to her, "Thank you so much for not having an abortion. Birth is all I needed from you. I'm fine, REALLY! I have a great life, and I hope you do too. Please let go of any guilt you may have from the choices you made about me." I never heard from her, but I never received the letter returned "undeliverable," so I assume it was received. I hope so.

My father is a different story. I tried for years to have a relationship with him and to earn his approval, but he is not interested in having a relationship with me. He has moved on and has a life that doesn't include reminders of what he did as a young man. It is sad that he is not interested in me or his grandchild, but it is his loss. In some ways, it is easier to live without the complications of having him and my mother in my life. I'm okay without them, and I wish them well.

IT'S NOT ALL ABOUT YOU!

When people say or do something that hurts your feelings, or when they fail to do or say something that you wish they would do or say, don't assume that they're inconsiderate or intentionally trying to hurt you. Ask yourself, "What are they going through that would make them act the way they did?"

Through all the years of feeling unloved, unwanted, used, and mistreated, I fine-tuned the self-pity through which I saw the world. I thought that anyone I let in would eventually hurt me, and I was usually right. I thought that if I did anyone a favor that they didn't immediately return, they were taking advantage of me. In those years, it never occurred to me that what other people said and did wasn't necessarily targeted at me. In other words, *it wasn't all about ME!*

Everyone faces challenges and adversity; everyone experiences pain; and even the most seemingly well-adjusted people may be empty, hurting, or dealing with their own challenges or adversity. Within the walls of what may appear to be the "perfect" family, there can be loneliness, sadness, anger, tension, and fear. Even these family members can experience the feeling of not being wanted and not being cared for, as well as the feeling of being unprotected and vulnerable. Although the depth of pain may not be terrible in comparison to someone else's standards, it may be devastating to the one feeling it, even in a "perfect" family. Most people will never mention their issues, but it would do us all well to remember that it's important to be kind to everyone because you never truly know what a person is going through.

DEALING WITH NEGATIVE EMOTIONS

If you are someone who is less than kind to the people around you, do something to deal with negative emotions so that you avoid taking it out on your spouse, children, friends, co-workers, or neighbors around you. You'll never have the level of success possible to you if you don't learn to treat people with respect. I am not saying you have to like everyone or agree with everything. But highly successful people treat others with respect and effectively interact even with people they do not like.

One way to deal with negative emotions is to see a good therapist, a pastor, or a friend whom you can really trust and to whom you can tell the things that happened to you that were the original cause of the anger. This can take the pressure off of you like taking the cap off a shaken bottle of soda. The release of the pressure of negative emotions can literally change everything.

Some people release the anger (or depression, which is just anger turned inward), pressure, tension, stress, or other negative emotions through physical activity, sports, or some form of art. There are various ways of dealing with negative emotions, including kickboxing, yoga, walking, reading a suspenseful novel, watching a movie that holds your attention, playing a musical instrument, painting, writing, or using some other creative expression. Others release their anger through prayer or meditation.

Others, like me, channel their anger into their work in search of that thing that has been called the ultimate revenge: success. You may have to try several different things before you find what works best for you. Regardless of what it is, find something that engages you. Be creative. Experiment until you find the right tension release for you.

When we live with negative emotions and feelings, it is much more likely that we will ruin the good relationships in our lives. Making decisions based on how we feel at the time is a mistake. Why? Because our feelings can change in an instant. We can be in a good mood, get cut off in traffic, and instantly be in a bad mood. Someone at work can snap at us, and suddenly we hate our job. Making decisions based on our feelings often leads to really bad outcomes.

For example, if my husband is going through a difficult situation and is grouchy, I can easily feel that he doesn't care about me; I may even begin to doubt that he loves me. If it goes on long enough, my feelings will tell me, *"I don't deserve this. I'm not going to take this. I'd be better off alone."*

Ultimately, those kinds of feelings can lead to giving in to temptation or just packing up and leaving. But if, instead, I assume something is bothering him or he's not feeling well, I'm more likely to be able to sympathize with him and do something that'll improve the situation. I should approach the situation from the standpoint of his feelings and what he's going through that is causing his bad mood, not my feelings and the effect his mood is having on me. Improvement in relationships comes from taking the focus off of ME and putting it on the other person.

AVOID NEGATIVE PEOPLE

After you decide not to take the bait and get angry or take offense, if you still often feel hurt, upset, offended, angry, left out, or rejected, you may not have surrounded yourself with the right people. This is data. Take the time to determine who's hurting you and how they're doing it. Is it because you're being too sensitive or is it because the people you're around are toxic? If they're toxic, get away from them, at least until they decide to treat you better.

When people are miserable and dishing out poison, it's a clear sign that they're dealing with serious issues. The reason why

We are influenced by our surroundings and the people around us.

someone is hurting you may not have anything to do with you at all. It might be some other circumstances or unresolved issues that have nothing to do with you. You just might be the nearest to the heat of the fire of their unresolved issues. If that's the case, move away from the fire rather than continue to get burned!

Unless you have worked through all your issues and have yourself at a place where you have dealt with all your "stuff," don't fool yourself into thinking that you can change the other person. Unfortunately, if we're not completely healed of the pains of our past, rather than us helping the other person up to our level, the hurting person will pull us back down into more pain.

As important as it is to choose the right role models and mentors, it's equally important to get away from people who are living wrong and making wrong choices. We are influenced by our surroundings and the people around us. If they're negative, we'll become negative. If they're moody, we'll become moody. If they have problems with anger, we'll start having problems with anger.

If you're around people who talk about using and selling drugs, you're likely to eventually be involved in using or selling drugs. Conversely, if you're around people who talk about investing and business opportunities, you'll start thinking about investing and business opportunities and eventually identify and act on those opportunities.

If there is any doubt that a person is a good influence, don't get into a close relationship with such a person, even if he or she says all the right things. Being in a relationship with the wrong person can literally ruin your life. Although that might sound dramatic, imagine being friends with someone who is involved in selling drugs, and you just happen to be there when he or she is arrested. You could have no involvement in or knowledge of the drug dealing, but you'd be arrested too!

Think of it this way: some people are safe to be with and some people should not be fully trusted. Determine which people in your life are "safe" and which can't be trusted. Then make an effort to spend time with the ones who are trustworthy. Do your best to be friendly to everyone, but keep distance emotionally and physically from people who aren't safe. People who are not safe include:

- People who are involved in illegal activity

- People who get drunk or wasted on drugs

- People who use you

- People who are angry much of the time

- People who will lie, cheat, steal, or talk trash

You may know people who fall into these categories. Some of the people you may have known your whole life, such as friends or family members from whom you can't imagine distancing yourself. You may think that these are the most important people in the world. You may think they will always be there. But the truth is that while some relationships do last a lifetime, others move in and out of our lives. In some cases, when a relationship ends, it's the best thing for us.

Naturally, the opinions of the people in your life now are important to you. Their likes and dislikes influence what you say, what you do, and what you are willing to try. But chances are that some of them won't be in your life five years from now. In fact, you won't even remember the names of some of those "important" people five years from now.

When I was a young girl, I was closer to the kids in my neighborhood than at school because they knew where and how I lived. In hindsight I know that we weren't really friends. They didn't care about me, but they were the only so-called friends I had ever known. I thought they were important. As time went by, one of them was shot execution style for choosing to use some of the drugs he had agreed to sell. One has been mentally ill since her choice to destroy her brain with drugs. One was convicted of murder. One joined a gang by passing the "entrance requirement" of shooting an innocent person. Another had a baby when she was 15, and that baby grew up to have a baby of her own when she was a teenager. To my knowledge, all three of those generations have been on some kind of government handout for years.

But by the time I was 12, I knew that if I was going to get out of that neighborhood and create a better life for myself, I had to get away from the influence of these people. My life is different from the lives of all those kids I grew up with because of the decisions I made versus the decisions they made. It's all about CHOICE. I CHOSE to work all day and study at night. I chose to do side jobs when I could find them and to wear the same clothes to work two or three days of every week. I chose to take my lunch rather than spend money on fast food. I chose to never smoke cigarettes or use drugs. During the time when I was making sacrifices for my future, many of the people I grew up with chose to smoke dope, live on welfare, complain, and feel sorry for themselves. Because they spent time together, they influenced each other, and all the bad choices they made were "normal" to them.

It is utter nonsense to think that somehow society is responsible for these people or that the government is responsible to take care of these "poor" people. These aren't "poor" people. These are fools who made bad choices. I feel sorry for them because they are pathetic losers, but not because some cosmic game dealt them a bad hand.

You may think I'm hard, cold, and callous calling those people I grew up with "pathetic losers." But they went to the same classrooms I went to, had the same teachers I had, and lived on the same street where I grew up. But when they went home at night, they had enough to eat. They went home to a house that had electricity, and they were able to take baths and showers. They had *"city toilets"* that flushed, so they were able to use the toilet any time they wanted to do so. Their clothes were purchased new and they were clean when they went to school. These people I'm talking about went home every night to a mother AND father living in the same house. If any of them were abused, it was not evident to me. No, none of them are victims of anything other than their own poor choices.

They could have had good relationships with the same teachers I had, but they chose not to do so. I'm grateful for the profound impact that my teachers had on me: my second grade teacher, Mary Bradford; the teacher who taught my third and fifth grade classes, Elizabeth Coffey; and that dear woman who taught me the business skills I used to fight my way up, Barbara Moyer.

I used to go through the old neighborhood every so often to remind myself of where I came from and to make sure that I never lost sight of how very far I've come. The last time I did that, I saw the gal who'd had a child in high school. She was in her forties, surrounded by her unemployed children. They are still living in the same house she'd grown up in; only now it was dirty and dilapidated. She told how she still started every morning by smoking marijuana. She didn't work and had no plans to try to find a job. It wasn't **living;** it was an existence – one that reminded me of the hell in which I grew up. I can't imagine choosing to live that way, yet because of the people they surround themselves with and are influenced by, many believe they have no alternative. I can't imagine what my life would be like now had I stayed in relationships with those people.

Determine not to allow anyone to move you away
from your desired outcome.

There are going to be some negative people whom you cannot completely eliminate from your life, such as mean-spirited friends, family members, co-workers, neighbors, or supervisors. There are also negative influences from characters on the radio, on television, in the movies, or on the Internet. When they talk, be careful what you listen to. Their negativity often comes in the form of whining, complaining, or criticizing.

If you must be around negative people, you have to work to balance the effect of their negativity in your life. You can do this by listening to an audio book on positive thinking or anything that is uplifting. Turn off any television, music, or video that has any negative or ugly connotation to it because this IS influencing your thoughts, words, actions, habits, character, and ultimately your future – whether you think it does or not.

Choose what you'll listen to, see, and be around. The quality of your life will reflect your choices. Choose ugliness and you'll have ugliness in your life. Choose positive influences, and your life will eventually reflect those influences. This advice is simple, but it isn't easy to follow because you're going to have to cut out some things and some people that you're accustomed to seeing. It'll be worth it, though; trust me.

A fish will only grow as large as its tank will accommodate. A five-gallon tank will allow limited growth; a lake allows much more growth; and the ocean holds the largest fish. It's the same with you. If you're in a small-minded group, you'll get small or limited results. With a better, more positive group of friends, you'll get better results. If you surround yourself with people who are disciplined, focused, positive, honest, kind, generous, and hardworking, you will eventually have those same traits, which are proven to contribute to success. We do literally become like the people with whom we spend time.

So even though you can't see negativity happening in your life, and you may think this isn't true for you, you will become negative and unhappy over a period of time if you're around negative, unhappy people. So be sure to intentionally spend time with people who are positive and who have the qualities you want to have. If you're in a close relationship with someone whom you have to get away from because he or she is NOT like the person you want to be, you must choose to spend less time with him or her even though it's difficult. You cannot allow anyone to hold you back from your destiny. You don't have to be mean or rude. Just spend less and less time with people who are complaining or being negative. Move on; move ahead.

It's been said that Thomas Edison, Henry Ford, and Harvey Firestone had vacation homes next to each other. It's not a coincidence that these brilliant, innovative people spent time together. They intentionally arranged to spend time together. Perhaps when they were together, they came up with ideas that they might not have had on their own. Enthusiasm and positive thinking are contagious. Anger, frustration, and gossip are contagious too. Which do you want to "catch"? Surround yourself with people who have what you want to "catch."

If you don't walk away from toxic people, you will "catch" what those people have. If you are toxic, you won't attract the right people in your life, and you won't get the good opportunities for advancement that you want. You won't grow to be the very best you can be. You'll stop your growth right where you are and may even go backwards.

Some people don't want you to get up out of your circumstances because they feed off of your weakness. They haven't pulled themselves up and out, and if you do it, it will be obvious that they failed. It's sad to think that rather than congratulate you on success, they would rather keep you down so that you are both down. These people would rather keep you broken by "doing things for you" such as providing drugs instead of helping you get clean. Then after keeping you dysfunctional, they'll usually expect you to do something for them in return.

This goes on only for so long before we get used to being lame and expecting people to give us something for free and to feel sorry for us. It's a mindset, a mentality; and if we don't change our thinking, we will miss so much of what life has to offer, so much opportunity, so much of the exciting, awesome things available to us.

As you make difficult decisions about avoiding or eliminating bad or unproductive relationships, remember that you came into this world alone and you'll leave it alone. The people you choose to distance yourself from may not love you at all. They may not even know what real love is. If they do truly love and care about you, they'll want you to have a great life.

YOU are the only one responsible for you and your choices. Don't blame anyone. Don't allow yourself to be influenced negatively by anyone else. Make your own choices and be able to live with the consequences of them.

We are often held back from BIG PLANS because other people in our lives are discouraging us and saying that our ideas are stupid or that they can't be done. When someone we care about, respect, admire, or submit to tears apart our dreams, it hurts in the moment, and it can negatively influence us for a lifetime.

Determine not to allow anyone to move you away from your desired outcome. If you are a doormat for people to walk on and you give up your wants and needs to do what others want you to do, or if you are influenced by the wrong people, you will miss your destiny, and your purpose. Later, I'll help you find your purpose. Your purpose is the source of your success in every area of life.

DEALING WITH BAD RELATIONSHIPS

Relationships with those of us who have been badly hurt can be difficult. We can be smart, ambitious, capable, loving, funny, and successful in our chosen fields of work, while at the same time we go in and out of personal relationships. In other words, we can be what the world would call "successful" in our professional lives and a total wreck in our personal lives. Why? Because the very things that helped us survive the dysfunction and succeed at work can destroy good relationships. We have to identify and refine or get rid of the techniques that helped us survive the dysfunctional environment.

What do I mean by this? When I was a young girl, I learned early on that if I cried and begged and pleaded while I was being beaten by my grandfather, the beating and yelling would be prolonged. Why? I'll probably never know. I learned by experience that if I stood straight with no emotion on my face and without responding in any way, the beating would be over sooner. Perhaps my grandfather got bored with punishing me or decided he wasn't getting the desired reaction and gave up.

This is terrible to admit – but to be totally honest, I learned that instead of crying, begging, pleading, or feeling sorry for myself as I stood there and took the beating, I could force myself to focus on something else. The only thing that worked for me at the time was revenge. I stood with my eyes narrowed and jaw set and thought of the death of the man who was hitting me. I could see him lying in a casket. I saw myself living a life without the constant threat of his anger hanging over my head. All the years of taking beatings without flinching and seeing my grandfather dead made me a tough, hard, take-no-prisoners person. My ability to "push through the pain" and do whatever had to be done has served me well in business. But the effect on my relationships, both personal and professional, is a different story.

My hard expressions and tough talk gave the clear impression to everyone in my life that I didn't really care if he or she stayed or left. I said things like, *"My mother and father both left, and I'm still standing. If you think I need you, you're kidding yourself."* I acted as though I couldn't care less about the person I was with. This was another survival technique. The truth was that I desperately needed to be loved and wanted, but I would never let anyone know that because I was afraid they'd use that vulnerability to hurt me.

What other survival techniques do we use? Here are a few:

- We do not trust anyone. It's a natural reaction for someone who's been betrayed to refuse to let anyone close enough to really hurt us again. We may say that we love the other person, and inside we desperately hope that the other person loves us. But we never really let him or her in because history has shown us that letting people get too close results in pain.

- We act as though hurtful words and actions don't bother us because the person isn't that important to us.

- We make jokes in an attempt to communicate that we are just fine or that we never really took the relationship seriously.

- We say the most hurtful thing we can think of either in response to the other person or to see if the other person cares enough to stick around. Some of us intentionally push to see how much the person really loves us. In our flawed logic, if a person puts up with a lot, he or she must love us.

- We are the first to leave or hurt the other person in a relationship. This comes from a deep sense that it's only a matter of time before the person I care about hurts me. People who have been hurt can't stand another rejection or abandonment, so they refuse to allow themselves to be vulnerable.

- We have been abandoned before, so we expect to be abandoned again. To avoid being taken by surprise, we often pick a fight, cheat, drink, do drugs, or do whatever else we know will destroy the relationship. Sadly, as a result we actually cause what we fear most.

I have known people who are very bright, highly educated, extremely accomplished, and fun to be around, BUT they have been married and divorced many times. Multiple failed relationships are evidence of unresolved issues. Many people seek the love, approval, and fulfillment they think the "right" person will provide. Unfortunately, they often commit to someone who has as many or more "issues" as they do or someone who isn't willing to deal with the neediness that comes along with someone who has been hurt.

Until you learn how to transform your old coping mechanisms into appropriate living skills for your new life, you will continue to choose the wrong people for relationships and participate in ruining relationships.

How do you end the cycle of failed relationships resulting from dysfunctional coping mechanisms? It is simple, but it is not easy. I know you can develop excellent relationships with good people because I have done so.

DON'T ALLOW OTHERS TO MISTREAT YOU

Those of us who were mistreated when we were young tend to go in one of two directions. We either let people walk all over us because we think it's normal and we want so badly to be accepted and loved, or we grow a hard shell exterior and decide no one and nothing will ever hurt us again. Either way, when you grow up thinking that unacceptable behavior is okay, it takes time to learn the truth about what is wrong and what is truly right. For example, if you grew up in a home where selling and using drugs were regular occurrences, it seems normal to you. If, as a child, you saw that conflicts were resolved by throwing a punch, you learned that the biggest, strongest person wins. Likewise, if people mistreated you, you might be willing to tolerate it now or you might mistreat others because you think it is normal.

If you are being abused, leave. If you have no friend or family to stay with, find a shelter, go to the police station, or go to a church and ask for help. I know that it is easier and more comfortable to dismiss bad behavior and stay in an abusive relationship. But if you do, chances are that the bad behavior will not change. This doesn't mean you don't forgive the person, go to counseling, and try to work it out. It simply means that you consider doing those things while keeping yourself and your children safe. If it's not possible to work things out, do yourself a favor: leave and forgive your abuser so that you can move on.

CREATING AND KEEPING GOOD RELATIONSHIPS

First, let's establish what a good relationship really is. A good relationship involves two people who are mutually committed to the well-being of the other. Good relationships take many different forms. What works for some is completely unacceptable to others.

For example, I know a couple who has been married for almost fifty years and lived apart more than they lived together. This is not because they didn't get along, but because the husband had jobs in different places and the wife didn't want to uproot their family and move. The husband would fly home on days off and they talked on the phone daily. They are retired now and are together every day. Their relationship worked for them.

Decide specifically what you want in your relationships. You, and only you – not your friends, family members, neighbors, or co-workers – can do this. For relationships with a spouse or close friends, decide the characteristics and qualities you want the person to have, the types of things you want to have in common, and very importantly, the things you're NOT willing to put up with. Be really specific about this. In this way, when people want to date you or try to be friends with you, you can compare them to your description of the "perfect person" for a spouse or friend and decide whether or not they match up with enough of the qualities on your list to give them a chance.

Of course, no one is perfect, so it's not necessary that the people you allow into your life have every single characteristic on your list, but it is important that they have the basics. Otherwise, the relationship is never going to really be satisfying to you, and you may very likely wind up in pain. You can save yourself a lot of heartache by not getting involved with the wrong person in the first place. Unfortunately, many of us settle for someone who is nothing like our ideal person because we assume we'll never be able to find anyone better.

We have to deliberately look for people who will not intentionally hurt us, who appear to make good decisions for their lives, and who seem to be a good influence on us. In all our relationships, we should endeavor to surround ourselves with people who have a positive outlook. It would be terrible to work hard on creating a good life only to have someone we care about ruin it.

It's important to remember that advice given to you by well-meaning people about what you should and shouldn't put up with may not be the best advice for your particular situation.

Now let's manage expectations. It is a mistake to believe the deception that love is a feeling. Love is NOT a feeling. It's a commitment. It's doing what you should do when you don't feel like it. THAT's true love. In our culture and with our language, we say we love our car, we love ice cream, we love this television show, we love some entertainer, we love our kids, and we love the person with whom we said we'd spend the rest of our life. This whole notion of saying we love someone and then some time later saying, *"I don't love you anymore,"* or *"I've fallen out of love,"* is sad and absurd. When we say this, we aren't using the word "love" the way it should be used.

Often we think that what we see of relationships on television and in the movies and what we read about in romance novels is the way things ought to be. No one could ever live up to those unrealistic expectations. Reality is usually quite different from the fantasyland produced in Hollywood. Real relationships that work are formed in many different ways. For that reason, it's important to remember that advice given to you by well-meaning people about what you should and shouldn't put up with may not be the best advice for your particular situation.

The truth is that even a well-adjusted, well-meaning person who loves you may occasionally mistreat and hurt you. As long as we're dealing with humans, we're going to experience pain. So, if we're going to experience success, we have to know how to decide what is acceptable behavior, how to hold people accountable to the behavior we will accept, how to say we're sorry when we screw up, and how to accept the apologies of others when they screw up. These are some of the relationship basics that don't get taught in dysfunctional environments. The good news is that these things can be learned at any age. With these things come improved relationships, and with improved relationships come joy – one of the key components of prosperity.

When someone says something that hurts or angers you, think about what was said BEFORE you reply. Decide to keep or discard what you've heard. If it's constructive criticism that you can implement that will result in making you a better person, a better parent, a better employee, etc., then take it in that context, make whatever changes you can, and move on. If what was said was just mean-spirited, ignore it. Simply pretend that it wasn't said. Decide to be "selectively deaf."

When decent people are irritable for a time or have unresolved issues that rear up once in a while, consider what they are going through. If their irritability persists or manifests itself in a way that is hurtful, find a way to hold them accountable. Start by telling them how their words or actions make you feel. Be specific. People don't respond to vague complaints. Tell them specifically what you want them to do or say differently. If, after you have told them what you want, they continue or repeat the hurtful words or actions, decide what consequences you are going to implement. Don't automatically jump to leaving or ending the relationship. For example, if you typically do laundry, prepare meals, or do anything

Had I acted on my feelings, I wouldn't be where I am and have what I have now.

else for some people, consider stipulating that until the situation changes, you are no longer going to do what they need done.

Most people are not trying to hurt you, but simply are thinking about themselves and their problems. Many people may not even be aware of the depth of the hurt they are causing you. Don't just run from the relationship. Clearly communicating your expectations and desires, holding the person accountable, and being willing to make changes the other person desires can bring lasting, positive change in the relationship. If the difficult time is the result of temporary circumstances, it will pass or change, OR you'll change and the hurtful things that person does won't bother you anymore. Your feelings may tell you to fight, leave, find someone else, or whatever... but CHOOSE not to act on those feelings.

Our feelings are meant to guide and lead us to good decisions about taking care of ourselves – physically, emotionally, and financially. The problem is that for some of us painful experiences have tweaked our feelings so that our "radar" is off kilter. Until we take control and recalibrate those feelings by getting therapy and/or having someone unconditionally love us into health and wholeness, our feelings are just as likely to lead us away from what's good for us.

If you say something that hurts someone, ask for forgiveness. It's not difficult. Try it. *Kiss and make up!* I know it sounds simplistic, but it works. If, after you've apologized, the person goes on and on about what you did or how badly he or she was hurt, offer to do something to make up for what you've done. Sometimes words aren't enough. On the other hand, if the person won't let this circumstance be resolved, remind him or her that you're sorry and you're willing to somehow make up for it; however, you're not going to be able to go back in time and undo what happened, AND you're not going to pay for it for the rest of your life. Ultimately, if people refuse to forgive you for something you've done wrong or something you failed to do or didn't do well, then it's their problem. They have to decide if they are going to allow this to ruin the relationship.

Just a word on accusations. Don't accuse people of wrongdoing. Ask questions, listen to answers, and be willing to give the benefit of the doubt. If you don't like the answer you receive, let them know what is acceptable and what will not be tolerated in the future. If you give an ultimatum, be willing to follow through with whatever consequences you've laid out.

If you are accused of something you did, tell the truth. Say you're sorry if what you said or did hurt the other person. If you can prevent the hurtful thing from happening again, say you will prevent it, and then do so. If you are accused of something you didn't do, tell your side and then confidently rest in what you know to be true, regardless of what people say or how they treat you. It doesn't matter what anyone else thinks of you or says about you. Other people's opinions of you don't change what is true.

HOW DO YOU DEVELOP GOOD RELATIONSHIPS WITH QUALITY PEOPLE?

Be the friend you would like others to be for you. Many people don't know the first thing about establishing a good relationship. Here are some guidelines:

- Make eye contact when you speak to people.

- Smile.

- Say positive, uplifting things to others. People like people who make them feel good.

- Don't be easily offended by things people say or do (or what they fail to say or do). If you're unsure of what they meant, give them the benefit of the doubt before passing judgment.

- Don't just write people off when they do or say something that you're not comfortable with.

- Be willing to do favors without expecting anything in return. For example, give someone a ride and share your lunch. If you have two coats and you see someone who doesn't have one, give him or her one of yours.

- Teach people what you know if they ask for help.

- Be patient with people. Decide what you're willing to do for others and what you're willing to put up with. Communicate your expectations clearly.

People want to be with others who are easy to be around. There are many negative people, so when people do get around a positive person, they want to spend more time with that person. This is true in the workplace as well. When bosses have a choice between two equally qualified people, they'll choose the one who is more positive because he or she is easier to work with. There's no telling how many good things will happen to you if you'll be the friend you would like others to be to you.

If you attempt to be a friend to someone, but he or she isn't interested, don't let it get to you. If you've done your best, the problem is with that individual. Move on to the next person. Eventually, you'll connect with good people.

There is a reciprocal relationship between the amount of love and/or respect we have for people and their ability to influence us or hurt us. Strangers can't deeply hurt you emotionally because you put little or no value in their opinion or you have the ability to put their criticisms into perspective. They don't know us; they could be crazy, ignorant, etc. But people we love, respect, and admire have the ability to hurt us deeply with their words and actions; they can influence us into making bad decisions, and they can break our hearts.

DO SOMETHING TO HELP YOURSELF

Don't wait for someone to come along and do something for you. Don't expect the people who have hurt you to come back and make things right. Usually they couldn't fix the situation even if they wanted to do so.

Feeling sorry for yourself won't move you closer to your goals. If someone feels sorry for you, it can feel good for the moment, but then what? Even when someone is moved by pity toward you, it isn't permanent. Even the most sympathetic friend in the world is eventually going to expect you to get over the pain and help yourself.

Sadly, the concern of some people may not be genuine at all, but rather a way for them to manipulate you to get what they want. Or they may be filling their own need to feel important by rescuing someone. In either case, attention from people who are filling their own needs will not move you closer to your goals. In fact, if you get stuck in a repetitive cycle of needing help and being rescued, it will hold you back from reaching your goals.

Refuse to feel sorry for yourself. You have to **decide** to stop feeling like a victim. Just make a decision that you will not feel that way one minute longer.

HELP FROM A THERAPIST

If you choose to find a therapist, invest the time in finding one who seems right for you. There are a lot of therapists who have the education and degree, but who aren't able to help you effectively deal with your particular issues. So, if you're not comfortable with one therapist, find a new one. Don't feel obligated to stay with someone if you are not getting results. That's not to say that you should never go back to someone who says something you don't like.

It probably won't be easy to work through some issues. The therapist may say things that you don't like, but you need to judge the person's character and the results of your sessions to determine whether or not the therapy is working for you.

There are three ways that I judge therapists. First, what is the quality of his or her life? Second, how does he or she conduct himself or herself? Most therapists are guarded about their personal lives, and rightfully so. But with today's access to information, we can use search engines to find information about lawsuits they've been involved in, articles written about or by them, and information posted on their websites and social networking accounts, in addition to doing basic due diligence, such as checking license status. If the therapist has made comments or behaved in ways that seem inappropriate, then he or she is probably not the therapist for you. For example, if I saw a social network posting that included vulgar language or drinking or smoking, I would question that person's judgment and not want them in a position of advising me. To clarify,

I'm not passing judgment on the person. I'm simply stating that I wouldn't want to make myself vulnerable to a person who didn't exercise what I considered appropriate judgment.

Third, how long does the therapist intend to work with you? There are people who have such deep-seated issues that years of therapy are required to resolve them, but many of us can see a good therapist and work through issues over the course of weeks or months, going back occasionally as things arise throughout the course of our lives. I have a psychologist friend whom I see a few times every two or three years as issues arise. I know it's time for "an attitude adjustment" when I catch myself angry or frustrated. Working through those things as they come up allows me to go to the next level in life.

Much of what we experienced as children makes no sense. So sitting in a therapist's office trying to make sense of something now that made no sense then is pointless. What is of great value is the understanding that the person who mistreated you was the one in the wrong. You were not at fault; you were a victim then. You are NOT a victim now. You are in control of your choices now, including the choice to forgive anyone who mistreated you. You do have the prerogative and the courage to act on those choices. And most importantly, you are responsible for the outcomes in your life from this point forward.

Dr. Viktor Frankl miraculously survived his time as a prisoner in the worst concentration camps of Nazi Germany during World War II. He watched as his friends, family, and neighbors were killed or died slowly of starvation, disease, or abuse. He survived being terrorized; he was forced to work almost literally to death; and he nearly starved in unspeakable conditions. He survived, and he went on to write, lecture, and practice a form of psychiatry he called *Logotherapy*. In his book, *Man's Search for Meaning*, Frankl tells of his experiences and how he survived. I strongly encourage everyone to read his book, especially people who are using the past as an excuse for their present and future circumstances.

The type of therapy that Dr. Frankl perfected after liberation from the concentration camps focuses on the future rather than on looking at the past and within, as is the case with other traditional psychotherapy. It leads us to consider the potential meaning of our lives and the sacrifice of suffering we've gone through. Frankl focuses on what can be fulfilled by us precisely **because** of the unique qualifications we have as a result of the suffering we have endured.

Focusing on the meaning of our existence shifts our thoughts and, consequently, our actions from pain to potential, from despair to hope. If you choose to seek therapy, search for someone who measures his or her success by your progress.

QUIT HURTING YOURSELF

Quit medicating yourself with alcohol, drugs, and nicotine. Use of these things is a way of medicating yourself so that you don't think about the pain. It doesn't make the cause of the pain go away; it doesn't move you closer to success; and it doesn't solve any problems. In fact, it makes them worse. I never used alcohol, drugs of any kind, or cigarettes because I thought it made people stupid. I valued my intelligence. In fact, I felt it was the only thing I really had going for me, and I wasn't going to jeopardize my primary asset. If you're medicating yourself with drugs, alcohol, or nicotine, get help immediately. You'll never really feel good and accomplish all you are capable of doing if you're putting poison into your body. Think of it this way: You might have been powerless to prevent people from hurting you in the past, but you DO have control over your body now.

Quit putting junk in your body. Putting junk food into your body is like putting vinegar into the gas tank of a car. The car may run for a bit, but it won't run long enough to get you where you want to go. Highly processed foods, meaning foods that don't resemble the way they were originally grown and foods full of sugar and chemicals, are what I am referring to as junk food. They may taste good and fill you up, but they will not fuel your body to accomplish all that you could if you were fueled by fresh, healthy food.

Drink water instead of soda; eat fruit instead of candy; chew "meal replacement bars" instead of cookies; and crunch on popcorn instead of potato chips. Eating junk makes you feel sluggish and lazy; it results in excess weight; AND it's expensive. Choose to put into your body only things that are going to give you energy, make you feel literally "lighter," and help you to take on the world, because that's exactly what you're doing. Don't blow off this advice. If you achieve outrageous financial success, but you're too sickly or don't live long enough to enjoy it, what's the point?

CHAPTER 6

TAKE CHARGE!

N ow at this point you may be hoping that I'll give you three easy steps you can implement by the end of the day that will get you a million dollars, or at least enough money to put you in a comfortable place to live, buy a nice car, and pay all your bills. Well, if I could do that, it would be magic. And there is NO magic.

A real friend tells you the truth. I am telling you the hard truth so that you'll take what I'm telling you, start doing it, and wind up with what you want and much more. You can. There is no reason why you shouldn't be able to make a list of just about anything you would like to have, start working toward achieving it today, and wind up having it all (and more) one day, as you enjoy your life and feel good about yourself the whole way.

TAKE CONTROL

You might be wondering how in the world you could possibly take control of anything. Well, consider the fact that you can immediately choose your attitude and your behaviors. You can choose what words you say, what you eat and drink, and even what you think. It might seem irrelevant to you, but taking control of these things can result in big changes in your life. It costs you nothing and requires no investment of time. It's simply a decision you make driven by exercising self-control.

I used to walk around with headaches and a nervous stomach wondering when the next awful thing was going to happen. For me, it wasn't a question of "if"; it was "when." Based on the *evidence* of my past, the next bad thing appeared inevitable. People who knew me commented that I'd had more bad things happen to me than most people have in a whole lifetime. That may describe your past too, but it doesn't have to describe your future.

I learned that who I was and what my life would be like tomorrow, next week, next month, next year, and beyond didn't have to be determined by what happened in my past. I learned that who I am and what my life is like tomorrow and beyond is determined by what I think, say, and do starting RIGHT NOW.

One seemingly irrelevant example of what I'm talking about is that once I was out on my own, earned a consistent paycheck, owned a home and had a nice car, I started drinking soda, specifically, Coca-Cola.

There had been no money for soda when I was a kid, so once I had the money, I started "treating myself" to this luxury. I told myself that I worked hard and deserved it. Before I was even aware that drinking this stuff had become a habit, I was addicted to it. I'd wake up every morning, stagger into the kitchen, and drink a bottle of Coke before doing anything. I drank the equivalent of 2½ six-packs every day for several years. I surrendered completely to my feelings and spent the money, whether I could afford to or not, to put that stuff in my body.

I did what I wanted to do rather than even trying to figure out what was right. As is the case with drugs, alcohol, food, sex, or any other kind of addiction, I was "medicating myself" and wasn't even aware of it. The caffeine and sugar helped me feel better, and without it I felt lousy. To add insult to injury, when I added up how much I was spending every month for this stuff, it totaled nearly $200 per month! I could have bought a lot of things that my daughter and I needed with that $200 each month.

As inconsequential as it may seem to others, it was a big deal for me when I decided to take control of this addiction. On July 11, 1987, I drank my last Coca-Cola. I experienced wicked headaches for about a month because of the caffeine withdrawals, but I pushed through and did what was right rather than what I desired. I knew I had to stop putting all that sugar and caffeine into my body. I knew it was right to quit spending my hard-earned money on stuff that wound up being flushed down the toilet!

What does all this have to do with success? Everything. I had to prove to myself I could take control of this trivial thing before I was able to believe I could take control of any of the big things in my life. (As an aside, in the month after I quit drinking Cokes, I lost twenty-five pounds.) I saved nearly $200 that I'd been spending on Cokes, and when the headaches let up, I began to feel better than I ever had. Less than two years later, I was in business for myself and loving it. That one little step of stopping my addiction to Cokes was the first step in proving to myself that I could control my feelings, which led to controlling my thoughts, which resulted in controlling my behaviors.

If you're going to have what you want in life, whatever that may be, you first have to take control of yourself and then your circumstances. Taking control starts with re-evaluating what you do, what you say, and even what you think. If you decide, for example, that you want to lose weight, the first step to making weight loss a reality for you can be taken immediately without costing you a nickel. You don't have to join a gym, buy special clothes or shoes, hire a trainer, or buy specially prepared food, although those things are great if you can afford them. The first step to losing weight is slowing down the movement of your hand to your mouth! Make a decision to stop putting the wrong food and too much food into your mouth. Get up and move your body. If your schedule doesn't allow for time to be set aside for exercise, make the effort to stand instead of sit and walk instead of ride where those are options. You can figure out how to get and maintain control if you want to badly enough.

Don't ever say that a habit or personality trait or physical condition is *who you are*, implying that it cannot be changed. It doesn't matter if everyone in your family is a certain way. You can take control and choose to be different. It may be true that you have to fight a natural condition that, if left unchecked, would slide back into place. But you can CHOOSE what you see, who you listen to, what you think, what you put in your mouth, and especially what comes out of your mouth.

If you say, *"I love smoking,"* you will never quit. If you say, *"My mom smoked, my grandma smoked, we're all smokers and that's it,"* then you'll never quit smoking because you see yourself as a smoker and identify yourself in a group of smokers. You can't quit until you can see yourself as a non-smoker. The same is true for your weight. If you're heavy and you say, *"I was a big kid, my dad is big, and grandpa is big. We're just big and that's how it is,"* then you'll never lose weight.

How do you see yourself now? How do you want to see yourself? How does the way you see yourself differ from the person you want to be? Some things you cannot change, such as your skin color, height, and shoe size. But the personality traits you have, the choices you make, the things you do, and the friends you have can all change.

You can take a similar approach to getting control over what you do to make money. Once you have figured out what you want your life to be like and what price you have to pay in terms of time and money to make that life reality, then you have to do the everyday work of making your goals reality. Reaching the goal doesn't happen overnight, although we all wish it would. The celebrations of achievement come after getting up and doing the necessary work every Sunday, Monday, Tuesday, Wednesday, Thursday, Friday and Saturday every single week. You may find yourself working all day and going to school at night or taking classes online during hours that you used to spend hanging out with friends or sleeping.

In my case, after I decided on a career in insurance, I wanted more than anything to be an owner because I knew that it was the agency owners who enjoyed the income and lifestyle I wanted. After working all day in the insurance agency, I picked up my daughter, cooked dinner, helped her with homework, helped her get cleaned up and get to bed, cleaned up the dinner dishes, did laundry, made our lunches for the next day, and then pulled out the books and started studying. After years of living on five or six hours of sleep, I got my insurance designation, which I thought would earn me credibility with my employer. I thought that having demonstrated my commitment to being the best, most knowledgeable agent I could be, they'd surely offer me ownership.

Years went by as I watched my employer hire new people (always men), give them the choice sales leads, offer them better compensation programs, pay all their expenses to attend conferences to help them find new clients, and provide them with customer service reps to help with their clerical work. Since I had been a customer service rep, I was expected to write my own letters, process my own service requests, and do all my own typing and filing, all while being expected to produce the same results as the men.

After being strung along for years by my employer, I could have felt sorry for myself because one more time I'd been taken advantage of or treated unfairly. But rather than resigning myself to dwelling on the unfairness, I decided to take action. I quit my job and started my own business. I knew nothing about running a business, but I was determined to learn what I needed to know to make my dream a reality.

I'd love to tell you that it was a "piece of cake." But the truth is, it was really difficult. I left a job that I'd had for almost seven years, and with it I was leaving a consistent paycheck, health insurance (after I'd just had surgery to remove cancer), a retirement plan, and co-workers I'd known for years. When I left this company, I was bound to a contract that did not allow me to take any of my former clients to my own business. I had to start all over in building relationships and getting insurance clients for my new business. This was a big risk because in the insurance business you can go months before actually earning any income, even though you have done hours of work for many prospective clients. So, I didn't know how long it would take me to earn the income I needed in order to cover even my basic living expenses.

The price was even more costly because just a few months earlier I had divorced my husband after learning that he was using drugs and had squandered our savings doing it. So, not only did I have no husband or family to support me emotionally or financially while I got the business going, my savings was gone. I had a little girl to raise, so leaving a regular paycheck seemed like an irresponsible thing to do. But at the age of 27, I started a business with no money, no financial support, no paycheck, no office, no employees, no brochures, and none of the office equipment necessary to do the job. There was a long list of things I didn't know how to do. But I KNEW I could take control of this and make my dream a reality because I had taken control of every other situation in my life.

I was scared, but I didn't let fear stop me from taking action. I want to really emphasize that point because a lot of people get to the place where they know what they want to do, but their fear of failure, fear of the hard work, fear of what other people will say, etc., keeps them from taking control of their actions and the situation to make their dreams reality.

I knew from growing up in an abusive environment that some fear is based in the reality that pain is about to be inflicted. As a child, I'd experienced physical pain that validated the fear that preceded it. As a young adult about to start my own business, I felt the fear of taking a risk like walking a tight rope without a safety net, but I knew that there was nothing that prospective clients or my former boss, or anyone else in business, could do to me that would hurt worse than what I'd already been through. I knew what real pain was, and none of these people could inflict it on me. The same is true for you. If you've experienced real pain, chances are that anything you'll have to go through to make your dream reality doesn't compare to what you've already experienced.

My boss laughed out loud when I gave him my notice to quit my job and told him what I planned to do. He reminded me that I had never run a business, and he smiled broadly as he ticked off items on the long list of all the things that I *didn't* know how to do. He ended the conversation by saying that he and his partners might consider hiring me back after I fell on my face.

He was right about that long list of things I didn't know how to do. But what he failed to take into consideration was the fact that I was in the process of taking control of my life and my circumstances, and that I was determined to learn all the things I needed to know to run a successful business. He didn't know about my past, so he didn't know the most important factor to my success – that I was a fighter. I'd fought to survive abuse, and I could certainly fight to build my dream!

In the years since May 3, 1989, when I started my business on the floor of my little condo, there have been many days when I didn't feel like going to work. A car accident some years before had left me with a 24/7 headache, so there were many times that I was in so much pain that I didn't think I could get up and go to work, meet with clients, go on a business trip, or make a presentation. But I pushed through the physical pain and through the feeling of not wanting to get out of bed. I did what I knew had to be done.

If people laugh at you, accuse you of daydreaming or wasting your life, or otherwise ridicule you, just smile and keep doing what you think is right. Don't engage in an argument. Let your results speak for themselves. If you have to say anything, just smile and say, *"You may be right. Time will tell."* Anyone who criticizes you is clearly not working toward anything more than what he or she has now. It doesn't matter what anyone else thinks of you or says about you. Twenty years from now these people will probably still be living the same way they're living now. You, on the other hand, will have systematically improved your life. The people who laughed at me, criticized me, ridiculed me, and said I'd never make it in my own business aren't laughing anymore!

Dignity and self-worth always result from true success, but not just from the final achievement of your goals and dreams. Your self-esteem will grow with every little success along the way. When you take control of what and how much you consume and you start to see the results of that control, you begin to feel better about yourself. When you're able to support yourself financially, you feel better about yourself. With every accomplishment that moves you toward your ultimate goals, your dignity and self-esteem rise. For me, once I emancipated and was supporting myself, I began to feel better about myself. I noticed that the more money I made, the better I felt about myself because I had accomplished my goals.

Don't make the mistake of thinking that the more things you have, the better you feel, because I can tell you from experience that this is not true. I have owned an 8,000-square-foot house on 34 acres with a 7-car garage full of every car I wanted, a house on the beach in Malibu, and a yacht in a Southern California harbor. All those things made my life more comfortable and enjoyable, but those "things" didn't give me dignity or make me feel better about myself. In fact, some of the most difficult times I've experienced in my adult life happened during the time I had all those things.

Some people aren't satisfied no matter how much "stuff" they ever have. Despite what they have, they don't have a sense of accomplishment about having accumulated it. That happens especially when things are accumulated through illegal, unethical, or immoral means or if the "stuff" came for free.

It's not wrong to want nice things, but make sure that part of your plan to get what you want includes building and maintaining your self-respect along the way. Never, EVER, compromise yourself to get something. If you do, you'll never be able to really enjoy it. Self-respect cannot grow inside you if you choose to do whatever *you want to make you feel good, all with the focus on YOU, YOU, YOU.* Self-respect grows from your own accomplishments, starting from the seemingly insignificant things like deciding to quit drinking soda, deciding not to eat chips, deciding to speak only positive words, helping someone without expecting anything in return, or whatever small step you can take right now to begin to get control of your life and influence your future.

While you're deciding what you want to do and have, realize that you're a complete and okay person without all the "things" you would like to have, and learn to connect your worth and value to who you are, not the "stuff" you have. As you check off the goals you've reached, your self-esteem will grow to the point where you feel really good about YOU – not just what you earn or what things you have, but about who you are as a person. When you feel good about who you are, that feeling will influence every area of your life!

Taking control means living deliberately
rather than by chance.

What does it mean to live deliberately? The majority of people just fall into their life's work because it just happened to be the particular industry where they happened to get hired. Many people go to work every day just tolerating or even hating their work, never having had the luxury of being able to step off the merry-go-round that is their life and really figure out what they're good at or what they'd really enjoy doing. Because most people increase their spending with every increase in income, they quickly become trapped in their line of work because they cannot afford to move into a different job or line of work where they would start out making less money. Consequently, they never take control and move toward the life they'd really like to live.

In a perfect world, we'd all have families who supported us emotionally and financially while we pondered why we were put on this planet, what our skills, talents, and abilities are, what bugs us that we'd like to change, and what the deepest desires of our hearts are. Then we could get the education necessary to be able to turn our dreams into reality. That would be nice, but that's not the way is it for many of us. So, while it's much easier said than actually done to live deliberately rather than by chance, you can make changes that will move you in the direction of your perfect life. Reading this book and implementing its advice is the first step to living deliberately.

It may seem completely impossible, or at least unrealistic, that you have any control over your circumstances and, further, that you could ever change them. But it's true. Remember, just because you don't understand something doesn't mean it isn't true. You probably don't understand electricity, but you know it exists every time you flip on a light switch. You probably don't understand all the science behind how you can stick a piece of paper into a fax machine in Los Angeles and have an exact replica of it come out just minutes later in Tokyo, or how cell phones or the Internet really work. The fact is that you don't have to have invented something in order to make it work for you. Whether you understand the concepts I'm giving you or not is inconsequential. They worked for me, they've worked for many others, and they'll work for you too. Rather than argue with what I'm saying or analyze it, just try it!

CONTROL YOUR THOUGHTS

> Our thoughts lead to
> Our emotions, which dictate
> Our words, which lead to
> Our actions, which result in
> Our habits, which shape
> Our character, which results in
> Our future.

If you want to change your future, you must change your character. To change your character, you must specifically choose your habits. To change your habits, act differently. To act differently, decide to speak differently. To speak positive words that lead to right choices, deliberately train yourself to think optimistic thoughts. *Don't derail this train by acting on feelings that don't line up with the person you choose to become.*

Taking charge of our lives and creating the results we want out of life begins with controlling our thoughts. It might appear to you that there is no way to control your thoughts. If that's the case, your thoughts are controlling you. It is possible to "take your thoughts captive," and in doing so, you will gain control of your words, which ultimately leads to being in control of your behaviors. One simple example of controlled thought leading to controlled behavior would be thinking things through before reacting. Controlling our behaviors is what gets us noticed for promotions, for new job opportunities, and in relationships with quality people.

When you change the way you think and feel, you generate different results in your life because better people are attracted to you. These are people who are less likely to intentionally hurt you. People who have been hurt or are hurting tend to be attracted to others who have been hurt or are hurting. Because they're hoping someone will come along and make them feel better and heal their hurts, they tend to have unrealistic expectations. When two damaged people get together, the result is two people who don't know how to love and give, who unintentionally cause more hurt for each other.

Even when you put a fairly well-adjusted person together with someone who's been severely hurt, the result is often that the well-adjusted person feels like he or she can't possibly keep the other person "fixed." He or she often leaves the relationship because it's just too much work.

When you have learned to control your thoughts, words, and actions, you will find yourself in relationships with people who are also in control. The result is that there'll be a lot less hurt in your life because you'll be in relationships with people who can control their urges to say and do hurtful things.

You may say, *"That sounds nice, but how can I control my thoughts?"* I hope that by now you have begun to change your thoughts like you change the channels on the television. Deliberately CHOOSE to think about what you want to think about, not what thought just popped into your head, not the bad memory that keeps replaying in your mind, not the ugly thing that someone said or did to you.

When you begin to CHOOSE your thoughts, you'll probably be surprised when you notice that the things you say change. Once you choose what thoughts you're going to allow in your mind and what words you will allow to come out of your mouth, remarkably, your actions will ultimately change too!

For example, if I say, *"I hate to exercise,"* chances are that even if I want to get in shape and make the decision to spend the money to join a gym, I will probably not stick with it. Why? Because I'm thinking thoughts about hating to exercise, saying words about hating to exercise, and then failing to go, which all demonstrate that I hate to exercise. If I say, *"I love potato chips,"* chances are that I'm going to think about them and wind up eating them. On the other hand, if every time I think about potato chips, I intentionally change my thoughts to something a funny comedian said or to a movie I liked, I'm no longer thinking about potato chips, and I am not as likely to eat them.

I hope this is making sense to you. If you can get this concept of deciding what you choose to think about rather than allowing every stray and random thought to pop into your head, it'll literally change your life.

When I was a little girl, I learned that I could endure being beaten if I thought of something else. I would close my eyes and see something in my mind that was different than the surroundings of the situation. Eventually, the scene in my mind helped me block out the sounds and the pain. Later in life that particular skill helped me in many ways. Because I could focus on something other than whatever pain or discomfort I happened to be feeling, I could push through pain and get to work when I didn't feel like going. I could think about my goals rather than the people and circumstances around me. I could close my eyes and literally "see" my goals in my mind as clearly as you can see this book in your hands.

One of the most important things I learned as a result of the pain of being burned with hot oil and cigarettes, of black eyes sometimes swollen shut so that I couldn't see what was coming next, and of a myriad of other injuries was that even in the midst of intense physical pain, emotional betrayal, and criminal cruelty, I had the ability to CHOOSE to think about something else. I learned that if I can do that during the trauma and the painful aftereffects, I can do it when co-workers are talking about me behind my back, when supervisors pass me over for promotion, and when people I love don't love me in return.

Begin immediately to think about what you're thinking about. Choose your thoughts carefully. When you notice that you are entertaining a negative thought, change the channel on the television of your mind and think of something else. Don't go around thinking that life has dealt you a bad hand, that people have treated you unfairly, etc. It's probably true, but it's also true for millions of other people. If you've been immersed in negativity your whole life, it may take a while to realize that some of the things you think of often are negative. Notice how you feel when you're thinking about something or someone. If you find that you're suddenly in a bad mood when earlier your mood was good, consider what or who you've been thinking about. Choose to think things like:

I am creative.
I succeed in everything I do.
I am able to accomplish everything I have to do.
I am strong.
I am courageous.
I am honest.
I have good character.
I am a good person.
I am a good friend.
I am a good employee.

Thoughts control our whole body, and I can prove it! When someone says something so funny that you laugh until your stomach hurts, your thoughts are what lead to your sore stomach muscles. Or when someone says something that makes you so angry or embarrassed that your blood pressure can go up and your face can get red, thoughts actually stimulated your heart to beat faster and controlled the flow of blood to your face. If you think of putting a wedge of a cut lemon in your mouth and biting into it, your mouth waters. It has been said that if we smell a wonderfully sweet thing and imagine eating it, insulin is released in preparation for our body taking in sugar – without ever actually eating the sweet thing we've smelled! Our mind powerfully controls our body. So, when desired images like the few I've mentioned above are focused on, *your body will respond to try to make it reality!*

To demonstrate that you can change what you think, try this experiment. Count silently, starting at one and going to twenty.

At some point in the counting, say your name. What happened with the counting? You had to stop when you said your name and then pick back up on the counting. It is not as though the counting went on when you spoke your name. The point of this exercise is to demonstrate that what you speak distracts you from what you are thinking. So, if you're thinking about something negative like a memory you'd prefer to forget, SPEAK something good – anything of a positive nature – because it will change the channel of your mind from the negative thought.

Make your mind your slave. When a negative thought comes to mind, you must train yourself to think about something else. Think about the way you WANT things to be, something you want, something funny, something you'd like to do with your future, a place you've been that you liked or some place you've always wanted to go. It doesn't matter which one of these things you think about as long as you are taking control and refusing to allow negative thoughts and images into your mind. This may sound unrealistic to you, but you can and must take control of what thoughts you allow yourself to have.

If you don't "change the channel," the negative thoughts that will bounce into your head will lead to negative emotions and will lead to negative results. Negative thoughts become negative feelings. Ugly, dark feelings lead to anger and/or depression.

Positive thoughts literally make you feel better. Therefore, you can overcome depression and anger by **choosing** to think positive thoughts. The more you deliberately do this, the easier it will be for you. Eventually, you'll do it without even thinking about it. Once you've trained your mind to think positive thoughts, those thoughts will show up on your face and in your choices. Ultimately that happiness and optimism will result in positive results like job offers, promotions, friends attracted to you because you're fun to be around, etc. Try it; you might be amazed at the results.

I predict that if you make this effort for thirty days, you'll never want to allow a negative thought into your mind again. Once you personally experience this phenomenon of negative thoughts and emotions moving you away from your goals and positive thoughts and emotions moving you closer to your goals, you'll understand the old saying, *"You cannot afford the luxury of a negative thought."* Think about it. If you take charge of your thoughts, you take control of your emotions. When you're in control of your emotions, you have control of your whole life.

About now you may be thinking, *"Okay, so what am I supposed to do when someone I care about says something ugly to me or about me?"* Well, what I'm about to tell you might not make any logical sense to you, but I can guarantee you that it works. Simply pretend the ugly words were never spoken or the careless or mean-spirited actions never happened. Act as though the person didn't get to you. Sound crazy? Regardless, it works. I'm not talking about ignoring physical abuse. It's important that appropriate boundaries be established in every relationship. These boundaries should be clearly communicated, relationship-appropriate, and mutually respected. An example of a relationship-appropriate boundary would be that you will never, under any circumstances, tolerate being hit by a boyfriend or girlfriend or spouse. Likewise, when mental abuse is destroying you, it must not be tolerated.

CONTROL YOUR MOUTH

Next, make your body your slave. Control your food. When your clothes start getting tight, eat less and move more. It's truly that simple. I know what I'm talking about here. I lost over 100 pounds in a four-month period of time, and I've kept most of it off for over twenty years by doing what I'm telling you here.

You can take control of the construction of your body and your brain cells by putting in that which will empower you – nutrients and water, NOT chemicals and preservatives. Want better results? Eat better. Get smarter, literally, by eliminating the toxins going into your brain. What toxins? Poisons like sugar, caffeine, nicotine, alcohol, drugs, and other chemicals.

THE POWER OF WORDS

Did people tell you that you were bad, ugly, fat, stupid, crazy, or some other negative adjective? Those weren't observations of truth. They were statements from abusive, dysfunctional, or simply misguided or mistaken people. It's up to you to decide whether or not those statements or predictions about you are going to be a reality in your future.

When I was growing up, I heard many ugly predictions about how my life was likely to turn out, and I could easily have gone in those negative directions. Thankfully, one man, the neighbor across the street from the little shack where I grew up, made a comment that he thought I'd be a millionaire by the time I was 30. Although I was only 7 or 8 at the time, I never forgot what he said. No one in my family had ever earned much more than minimum wage. Although it seemed completely impossible at the time, I chose to believe it was possible. I tried to put all the ugly comments and predictions that were said to me and about me out of my mind, and I focused on that one statement of that one man for many, many years until finally it became a reality.

You may be thinking that you don't know of anyone who has ever said anything good to you or about you. That's okay. Make your own positive prediction. Think about what you want and predict that you're going to have it within a specified time. It doesn't matter who makes the positive prediction; the point is that a positive outcome gets introduced into your mind. Once that happens, your brain can begin to think about ways to make it a reality. Your brain can be doing this while you're working, watching television, even while you're sleeping.

Instead of hearing negative things in your head, tell yourself, "I can do anything I decide to do. It's only a matter of time before I get my big break. When opportunity comes my way, I'm going to be prepared to take advantage of it. I am smart. I am attractive. I am a winner." Sound crazy? To some people it might, but SO WHAT?

This is not "New Age" psycho-babble. Positive self-talk is a proven technique that costs nothing and can be implemented immediately. Olympic athletes have done this for years. They talk to themselves, encourage themselves, meditate on winning, and visualize themselves successfully completing the tasks necessary to win and accept their gold medals.

People who are wildly successful know that they cannot allow the only encouragement they receive to come from others. You can't count on someone always being in your life who is able to get past his or her own circumstances to encourage you. Many times the people in our lives have bigger issues than we do, and if we listen to their negativity, it'll bring us down rather than lift us up.

Visualize yourself doing what you want to do, having what you want to have, and living the life you want to live. This presupposes that we know what we want. We can see it in our mind's eye, and we don't doubt that we're going to have what we envision. This positive visualization and talk of what you want has been proven effective, and it works if you do it correctly and consistently. I'll talk more later about how to figure out exactly what you want. But before you can do that, you must begin now to use positive self-talk and visualization to "undo" the hurtful words and actions that hold you back.

The power of our words cannot be emphasized enough. This particular point could be expounded upon to fill a separate book. To illustrate the power of words, consider that some years ago a culture was discovered where no one had ever divorced. When people married there, they stayed together for life. When researchers studied the people and their culture, to their surprise, they learned that these people had no word in their vocabulary for divorce. It just didn't exist for them. They could not say it; therefore, they didn't do it!

In our culture, on the other hand, divorce often starts with one person speaking the "D" word in anger, fear, or desperation. Once it's been said, it's easier to say it again. After it's been threatened, both people consider it as an option, and often one of the two people eventually acts on that option. I suspect that many times it is because one of the two threatened divorce if some action happened "one more time." When the "one more time" threat happens, pride forces the person who made the threat to back it up with action. The next thing you know, they're divorced.

To use another kind of example of the power of words, on several occasions I've had the experience of telling people the way I hoped things would turn out before I knew with certainty that it would go that way. I'm not talking about lying or exaggerating, but about carefully choosing your words so that you talk about the future you want to create rather than the future that you dread. Time after time I've seen things work out exactly or very close to the way I expected they would.

Coincidence? I thought so the first two or three times it happened, but not when this happened over and over again. It's not coincidence or luck. It's the deliberate practice of saying things that are not as though they were. It's hopeful rather than hopeless. It's being positive rather than negative. It looks to the future as a good time when things will be better than they are today rather than dreading the future. For example, if you don't have the money to buy something you need or really want, rather than saying, *"I can't afford it,"* you might try saying, *"I'm not in a position to buy it YET, but one of these days it will be mine!"*

When I was just learning to speak of things the way I wanted them to be rather than what they were at present, I had no money because I had just started my business. In my condo I had no furniture, no refrigerator, and no bed, so I was sitting, eating, and sleeping on the floor. If I had told my little girl that we couldn't afford this, and she couldn't have that, I would have become depressed and discouraged, and that attitude would not have helped me grow my business. No one wants to do business with someone with a bad attitude. Regardless of whether or not we had food to eat, I had to maintain a positive, upbeat frame of mind. So, when we had to do without something that we needed or wanted, I'd say, *"I don't have money for it now, but one day we'll be able to buy anything we want!"* Those words ultimately became reality for me.

Words are evidence of what's in our hearts. Angry words show that there is anger in our hearts. Hurtful words show hurt in our hearts. Jealous words show jealousy in our hearts, and so on. What we want to have in our hearts and show in our lives have to come out of our mouths. Regardless of how we act, our words reveal the secrets in our hearts. So, if we want to appear confident, strong, courageous, trustworthy, and dependable, we have to say words that prove that we are what we want to be.

The power of your own words can work against you just as easily as for you. Begin immediately to pay attention to every word you say. When you catch yourself saying something negative about yourself, someone else, your employer, or your circumstances, **stop**. Either don't say anything at all, or rephrase what you were saying to sound hopeful that the negative person or situation will soon change. You may not think you can control what you say, but you can. In fact, you're the only one who can.

Ugly, profane, coarse, vulgar language is a sign of immaturity, ignorance, and/or lack of education. Use of inappropriate language will eliminate you from many opportunities. Every time you open your mouth and allow a vulgar word to come out of it, you're telling the world that you don't know an appropriate word for expressing how you feel or what you're trying to communicate.

CHOOSE to shake off every unhealthy thing
ever said to you or every unhealthy comparison
ever made about you.

Listen more than you speak. You'll be amazed at what you'll learn and how many opportunities will come to you if you'll listen for them. Too often we dominate conversations when, if we'd just listen, we'd learn information that would move us closer to our goals, provide opportunities for making extra money, save money on something we need, or make our life easier in some way.

Develop the habit of speaking well of others. If you can't say something good about someone, then don't say anything at all. Truly successful people do not gossip; or say things that are untrue, unkind, unfair, or negative; or speak about things that are illegal, immoral, or unethical.

For every bad thing you want to say, think of an opposite positive statement and say that to yourself – even if you don't believe it. Keep saying this positive statement about yourself, others, or your situation. Eventually you will believe it, and ultimately it will be true. If you are uncomfortable about talking this way in front of others, say it silently in your head, whisper it, or say it in the bathroom with the water running! Put it on a piece of paper and read it first thing in the morning and last thing at night and several times throughout the day until you truly begin to get it in your head and your heart.

Don't ever say things that start with "*I don't deserve... ; I can't afford... ; or I shouldn't have... .*" It may be true that you don't have the money or that it wouldn't be wise for you to spend money on a certain thing right at the time you decide you want it. BUT don't confuse making wise decisions about money and the timing in which you'll spend or invest your money with the thoughts that you don't deserve the thing or that you shouldn't have it. You deserve everything that you earn. That's the beautiful thing about EARNING your living. Along with monetary compensation, you get experience, education, expertise, and the dignity and self-esteem that you can't get any other way.

The point of all this is that, very simply, if you predict a bad thing, that's probably what you'll get. On the other hand, if you predict good, you're much more likely to get good results. So, PREDICT GOOD!

In my life and in the lives of many people who have overcome adversity, there have been times when whatever level of hope we had was <u>all</u> we had. It's important to build on what you have and remain hopeful regardless of how little you have or how impossible the situation may seem. In some other languages, the word "hope" means much more than the way we think of it in the English language. For us, it is almost synonymous with "a wish," which is not likely to become reality. But hope is so much more than a wish. It is **fervent expectation**, the same as your expectation that the sun is going to rise in the east in the morning and set in the west in the evening. You don't *think* the sun is going to rise. You KNOW the sun will rise. In the same way, don't just wish for what you want, but EXPECT to have what you want.

Once we decide what we want, it's important that we begin to speak as though we will one day have the thing we desire. We must eliminate from our vocabulary any negative thing that would make it sound as though we don't believe what we are saying. We have to believe that what we're saying could become a reality, regardless of how unrealistic or improbable our desires may sound. *No one else can do this for you.*

It might not sound realistic for you to begin to say that you're going to be a millionaire, especially if you don't have a job, a permanent address, or transportation. So start with talking about something you can believe. For example, you can say that you are going to have good friends you can count on. You can say that you're going to have a great family. You can say that it won't be long and you will have transportation, or you will have a great job soon. I say things like this:

> *My words are powerful, and they become reality.*
> *I speak only positive words about myself, others, and circumstances.*
> *I accomplish everything I decide to do.*
> *I make right choices.*
> *I treat people right.*
> *I am smart.*
> *I am a good person.*
> *I deserve good things.*
> *I am here for a reason.*
> *I have a unique set of skills, talents, and abilities that are exactly what is needed to accomplish my purpose.*

All of us see things through the prism of glasses formed by the beliefs, understandings, and misunderstandings of our life experiences from childhood through the present. Through self-talk and visualization we change the distorted beliefs and understandings we formed as young children. By talking positively to ourselves, we are replacing the lenses in those glasses that were forced on us so long ago with lenses that help us see our lives in the positive, hopeful, encouraging, victorious light that we should be seeing in our lives.

Positive self-talk will help you move on and away from painful memories and poor choices in your life. You do not have to spend your whole life as a victim of what has happened to you. This is one thing you can do right now that requires no money, no special training, and no equipment. It works. Try it.

ACTIONS AND HABITS

Everyone is known in his or her group, family, or workplace for something. Some people are known as the one who is *sick all the time*, the one who *complains all the time*, the one who *gossips*, the one who is *angry all the time*, the one who is *moody,* and so on. Some people are known as the one who seems *happy all the time no matter what happens*, the one who is *always in a good mood*, the one who is *always working*, the one who *always has money*, the one who *always looks good*, the one who *wears nice clothes*, or the one who *drives a nice car*. You get the picture.

So what *are* you known for? What do you *want* to be known for? How are those two things different? If you want to be the one known for always being in a good mood, then choose to be in a good mood. It doesn't have to cost you anything to create a reputation for yourself as the one who is happy, the one who is always smiling, the one who is very organized, etc. Create your own reputation by describing yourself and acting the way you want to be and the way you want to be known by others.

Once you have an idea of the way you want to be and be seen by others, make your body your slave and force yourself to act in ways that are consistent with the *new you*. This means controlling your actions so that they line up with your newly controlled thoughts and positive words.

> *Create your own reputation by describing yourself and acting the way you want to be and the way you want to be known by others.*

You already know the importance of making the decision to treat people appropriately *even when they don't deserve it.* It will be difficult at first if this is very different from the way you and the people in your life have acted. But the more you are able to control your thoughts and words and the more you practice doing the things that you know you must do, the more your actions will become habit. Eventually, your habits become incorporated into your normal behavior and become part of your character. You'll find eventually that you no longer do things that are out of character for the *new you*, and it's no longer even an effort to do the right things.

ELIMINATE BEHAVIORS THAT DON'T FIT THE NEW YOU

Many of the inappropriate language and behaviors I carried into adulthood were coping skills I acquired while trying to survive abuse. Although many of those coping skills helped me through very difficult times in my personal life and in the workplace, some of them resulted in me being hard, overbearing, opinionated, and easily offended.

When I was angry, depressed or withdrawn, friends and co-workers would say things like, "*What's the matter with you?*" I had no idea what was wrong with me or how to change it. People who asked me that and similar questions upset me more. I didn't know how to be any different than I was. The problem was that now that I was an adult living and working in a "normal" environment, the words and actions that served me well in childhood were entirely out of place. For example, the foul mouth and "bad-assed swagger"

There are things that may be a natural tendency for you, but you have control over whether you continue to allow those things to be a part of your personality.

that served me well while walking through my neighborhood of bikers and gang members didn't translate well to the professional environment of an insurance agency!

Like the negative behaviors we covered earlier, many people accept aspects of their personality as something that cannot be changed. They say things like, "*Everyone in my family is like this,*" and make no effort to change. There are things that may be a natural tendency for you, but you have control over whether you continue to allow those things to be a part of your personality. I know this is true because I heard from many people throughout my childhood that I looked like my mother, acted like my mother, and would turn out just like my mother.

I was told that I laughed like she laughed and had other characteristics that reminded people of her. In the few times I've seen my mother, I saw her laugh once, and I'll never forget it. I watched the way her eyes crinkled and listened to the sound of her laughter.

It makes me smile even now as I think about it. When I was a child, I thought my mother was beautiful and faultless. I thought she would eventually come back for me. So I held on to those similarities that people pointed out. I wanted to look like her, act like her, and be like her. So, until I began to learn the value of deliberately creating the personality I wanted, I wasn't even interested in changing. The similarities to my mother were the only connection I had to her. Unfortunately, being like someone who was, in truth, far from faultless was holding me back from the future I wanted. My life began to change for the better when I began to create the person I wanted to become.

Using the suggestions included here, I decided who I wanted to be. Then I systematically identified and eliminated the words and behaviors that were not consistent with the person I wanted to become, and I added words and behaviors that were. In doing these things, I recreated my personality into who I wanted to be.

CHARACTERISTICS THAT MUST BE DEVELOPED IN ORDER TO ACHIEVE SUCCESS

I have read over 600 books on business, psychology, self-improvement, and positive thinking. Many are written by or about exceptionally successful people, some of whom are mentioned in this book. One theme that runs through all of their lives is that you will not earn lasting, genuine prosperity if you do not develop these character traits:

> **Honesty and integrity**
> **Loyalty and faithfulness**
> **Courtesy and manners**
> **Kindness and gentleness**
> **Work ethic**

Self-control (especially your temper)
Perseverance

In addition to these character traits, it's important that we learn from every setback and failure. Some of these characteristics, if developed out of balance with the others, can create problems. But when they are developed in balance with each other, they make you much more powerful than you are now. It sounds simple, which it is. But don't confuse being simple with being easy. Some of these characteristics are self-explanatory. Others, like work ethic and persistence, may require some understanding before you can begin to develop them. All of them are a choice.

WORK HARD

The root of work ethic, which I'll talk more about later, is being a hard worker. Specifically, this means forcing yourself to do the right things and to work hard when you'd rather do something else.

People who are lazy will NEVER enjoy all
five points of genuine prosperity, which are health, joy,
peace, good relationships, and financial stability.

You have the later years of your life to sleep late or do whatever it is you want to do. If you do what I'm suggesting throughout this book, eventually you'll be able to afford to do whatever you want to do. Work while your body and mind are able to do it. Those who are willing to work long and hard will get ahead of those who would rather kick back, relax, watch television and sleep late. People who are lazy will NEVER enjoy all five points of genuine prosperity, which are health, joy, peace, good relationships, and financial stability.

To take control of your life and get the results you want, you have to change your actions and reactions. Your ultimate success will depend on the degree to which you can replace any tendency to be lazy with hard work.

PERSEVERANCE

You might be saying, "*Why do I have to work so hard when others came from loving families, got a college education, inherited the family fortune, or eased right into a comfortable job in the family business?*" Well, hold on; this is profound: **IT'S NOT FAIR! Period!**

Many people started the race of life as though they had a fifty-pound bag of sand strapped on each ankle and they were five miles behind everyone else who began at the starting line, wearing all the

---

Perseverance means that, regardless of your past or how many bad things happen to you, you continue to make the effort to control your thoughts, your words, and your actions.

---

right gear and having an adoring fan handing them a cup of cold water every quarter mile.

Some give up and feel sorry for themselves for the rest of their lives. Some medicate their pain with drugs or alcohol. Some bring on, or exacerbate, illnesses or injuries because this lets them off the hook of the expectations of others or the achievement of their own goals.

BUT some keep on trying. If they get knocked down seven times, they get up eight. If they get fired or laid off, they go right out and find another job without hesitation. The ones who refuse to give up are the ones who will ultimately be okay, or to paraphrase a childhood saying, "Last one to give up wins!"

The world is full of people who gave up, but the world is changed by people who try again after they've failed.

Walt Disney is said to have filed bankruptcy several times before successfully starting Disneyland, which is now a household name and billion-dollar empire.

Colonel Harland Sanders didn't even start Kentucky Fried Chicken until he was 65 years old! When he was going from restaurant to restaurant trying to sell his recipe for fried chicken, there were those who called him a failure. So, anytime you start thinking it's too late for you, remember Colonel Sanders and the fact that there probably isn't a good-sized city in America that doesn't have at least one KFC!

Abe Lincoln, who some say was the best United States president ever, had no college education, lost election after election, suffered a nervous breakdown, and finally was elected President. He saved the United States from division, ended slavery, and founded the Republican Party.

Cervantes, who at 53 had been in prison several times, had a series of failed government jobs and lost the use of his hand in a war injury before he wrote the book, *Don Quixote,* which is still of interest to readers more than 350 years later!

There is a story of an old donkey that fell into a well and couldn't get out. The donkey made horrible noises in the hopes that it would be rescued. The farmer couldn't get the donkey out, so he asked some of his neighbors to come help. They tried everything and couldn't get the donkey out of the well.

When all else had failed, they decided to shovel dirt in on top of the donkey to bury him and put him out of his misery (and to stop the horrible noises the animal was making). The farmer and his neighbors started shoveling dirt in and the noises got louder and more frantic, almost as if the donkey were screaming. They kept shoveling. After a while the noises stopped, so they figured the donkey was dead. They kept shoveling to completely fill the hole and soon, much to everyone's surprise, one the neighbors looked down and saw the donkey's head!

It seemed that after struggling and screaming, the donkey decided that no one was going to help him, so he became resourceful and began to step up on every newly shoveled mound of dirt that came into the well. As they shoveled, he'd shake off the dirt and take a step up. He did this until, finally, he stepped right out of the hole and walked off.

Just like that old donkey, you can persevere by building the steps to your future using the bricks people have thrown at you! Don't succeed **despite** what you've been through, succeed **because of it** – because nothing anyone can do or say to you now is likely to hurt anymore than what you already experienced.

Perseverance means that, regardless of your past or how many bad things happen to you, you continue to make the effort to control your thoughts, your words, and your actions.

When you make a mistake and catch yourself in a wrong thought, catch yourself with negative words coming out of your mouth, or find yourself doing something you know won't help you become the person you want to be, just stop and decide that you won't do it again. Be like a pilot who makes flight corrections to compensate for weather, wind, turbulence, or other aircraft and arrives safely at the desired destination. Keep trying to do the right thing, and YOU WILL SUCCEED.

CHAPTER 7

PREPARE YOURSELF FOR SUCCESS

P repare yourself so that when opportunity comes along, you're ready. In my case, I worked hard to learn how to type accurately over 100 words per minute and to take shorthand at about 120 words per minute. At the time that I was learning and practicing, I invested a lot of time and energy without earning any money. But when the opportunities that required those skills presented themselves, I was ready. Had I not had those two skills, the opportunity to work at the insurance agencies and to take minutes at the homeowner association meetings would have gone to someone else, and my life might be very different today.

Whatever you've been through in your life has contributed to how you feel about yourself now. How you feel about yourself influences how you talk about yourself. How you see yourself and talk about yourself influences how other people see you. For many years I thought of myself and described myself as a "white trash ghetto girl." I said, "*You can take the girl out of the ghetto, but you can't get the ghetto out of the girl.*" When I said those things, I was literally telling people that I wasn't prepared to receive success. Eventually, though, by changing the way I thought, most of the things I said, and the things I did, I realized that I am not that "white trash" person anymore.

Sadly, I'll never know what opportunities I missed because of the way I thought and talked about myself. I'll never know how many promotions, customers, and new business opportunities I lost because others didn't want a "white trash" friend, employee, insurance broker, or business partner.

Part of preparing yourself for success is avoiding choices that will automatically eliminate you from jobs and other opportunities because, like me calling myself "white trash," you'll never know what people and opportunities are passing you by. People will usually not take the time, make the effort, and risk confrontation by telling you the real reason they have chosen NOT to hire you, to be friends with you, to promote you, or to do business with you.

For example, potential employers may thank you for your application and tell you the job has been filled. In reality they desperately need to find and hire people who will do a good job and present themselves properly to the public, but they feel they cannot hire people who have tattoos on their necks and piercings in their noses, or who use vulgar language. They will just choose someone else. Having a tattoo that cannot be covered up or failing to choose the right words for the right situation are not worth what you could be losing. You don't know what you don't know. *Think about it.*

CHOOSE YOUR MENTORS AND MODEL
THEIR BEHAVIORS

To position yourself to receive the specific successes you want in your life, consider what attitudes you have that must be adjusted before you can be the person you want to become. Before you can change what people think of you, you have to change what YOU think of yourself. You must see yourself differently and not ever say anything about yourself that is contrary to the *new you.*

Is there someone you know whom you respect? If so, model yourself after that person. You may want to choose a number of people to model. Many of us have heard the advice not to copy others. *"Be yourself." "Be an original."* That's good advice. Although what I'm telling you now may sound contradictory to this advice, stick with me and allow me to explain how you can become the best YOU can be.

You might be thinking, *"She's talking about being a wannabe."* That's exactly right! Whatever things have been done to you and whatever choices you have made, good and bad, all added up to make you the person you are, and it didn't happen overnight. You cannot undo the past, but you can intentionally change who you are now so that you can be who you design yourself to be in the future. Changing into who you want to be won't happen overnight. It takes time. It can and will happen if you make it happen.

Some people say, *"I am who I am, and I can't change."* It is true that your nationality, your past, your education, and your family are what they are. Those things are all part of who you are today, but good or bad, they do not have to determine your future. By choosing what you think, what you say, and what you do, you are intentionally creating your personality, your character, your reputation, and your future lifestyle.

Uncomfortable with the thought of "acting"? Most people have had the experience of trying to act cool, or trying to act a certain way to fit in with a particular crowd. Young people have been dressing and styling their hair like their celebrity idols for years. The fashion industry banks on people choosing to dress like models wearing "this season's" designs. Once you identify the way your role models act and begin to act like them, flavored with your individual personality, you WILL fit in with truly successful people.

While some say, *"People don't change,"* that's simply not factual. Yes, some people choose not to change, but there are many people who have made amazing turnarounds in their lives. I'm one of them. I'm proof that it can and does happen!

To take the first step toward becoming the person you would like to be, visualize yourself the way you want to be. Visual images can be extremely powerful, so consider getting pictures of people looking the way you want to look or doing what you'd like to be doing. If you have access to a computer, you can find an image of someone you want to be like or someone doing what you'd like to be doing and cut and paste your face onto that picture. Then look at it first thing after you wake up and last thing before you fall asleep. The more you can customize the image of who you want to become, the more powerful it will be.

For me, significant change took place when I began to intentionally copy the behavior of people I liked and respected. I chose my role models and took note of the way they acted by watching them and reading about them. The first major change came when I chose to emulate a type of person I referred to as a "church lady." These were ladies who seemed nice and approachable, never argued or got into any conflict, were always pleasant and positive, and had a reputation for helping others. All those were qualities I wanted to have. I watched the way they conducted themselves, listened to what they said, took note of things they would never say, and then began acting like a "hardworking, respectable *church lady.*"

At the same time, I was watching and listening to my boss, who was a very successful businessman. I intentionally began to read the books he read, to say the kinds of things he said (which were always positive and hopeful), and to act the way he did with clients.

One day I realized I had become a hardworking, respectable "*church lady*" and business person. I had become who I had been trying to be! I no longer even remotely resembled the "white trash ghetto girl" I had been and that some people expected me to be. And, I had proven wrong all the people who predicted that I'd be "just like my mother."

You may be asking, "*How, specifically, did that happen?*" Well, it began with me making the decision to talk, dress, and act differently. Once I did that, things started to happen. Specifically, one of my insurance clients was a hair stylist. This stylist and her sister, also a business person, were successful people and were well put together, meaning their outfits, hair, and make-up were always perfect. When they offered advice about my hair, make-up, and clothes, I listened carefully because I wanted to be professionally "well put together" like them.

I was receptive to their advice, which evidently gave them confidence about taking some pretty dramatic steps to help me. One day when I met with them to talk about their business insurance, one of the sisters sat me down in one of the salon chairs and started cutting off my hair! Tears rolled down my cheeks as I watched my long hair fall to the floor, but I wasn't crying later when my business improved as a result of me having a much more professional look.

About a week after my new hairstyle was "forcibly imposed" on me, the sisters called me in for another meeting. When I arrived this time, one of the sisters told me to get in her car. Instead of going to lunch to talk about their insurance, as I thought we were doing, she pulled into the parking lot of her favorite clothing store! I followed her around like a puppy while she literally picked out clothes for me that would *accentuate my positives and mitigate my negatives*. I was red with embarrassment as she followed me into the dressing room and told me to try on the various outfits.

But I did as she said. One by one, she'd hang them outside or set them aside for purchase. My stomach was churning the whole time because I knew I didn't have money for clothes like this. Each price tag was more than the next. Silk blouses, wool suits, belts and scarves to match – I thought I was going to throw up.

After she'd selected ten things that could all be mixed and matched to make almost twenty different outfits, we stood in line at the cash register. I was sweating at the thought that my credit card was going to be declined. Remarkably, the charge went through, and I left that day with a totally new wardrobe and a completely different look. Because those two ladies took a personal interest in me, I looked and, surprisingly for me, *I acted* more professional. I started to believe that I was the person I looked like – a professional businesswoman.

Another insurance client casually mentioned one day that she never left her house without a matching handbag and shoes. Although it was a trivial thing, I incorporated that little guideline into my life because it "fit" with the model of the professional businesswoman I was trying to become. I have carefully paid attention and incorporated every other little guideline that "fits" the person I want to be. When I see or hear someone who knows more about a subject than I do, I listen carefully to what they say for little bits of advice I can incorporate into my life. I hope to be learning and improving for the rest of my life. I hope you will too.

As long as I still thought of myself and referred to myself as a "white trash ghetto girl," I made the kinds of decisions a "white trash ghetto girl" would make. The decisions about who I chose to have relationships with, the way I interacted in those relationships, the language I chose, the way I dressed, and the things I thought were entertaining were all from the perspective of a "white trash ghetto girl." When I began to CHOOSE who I wanted to be and how I wanted to act, I began to change what I thought about. After a while, I began to see myself as a different, better person. It was then that I realized that I was no longer *acting* like someone else. I had *become* someone else.

The money, businesses, houses, office buildings, cars, vacations, and all the rest didn't transform me. Those things were acquired <u>after</u> I changed. What changed me was <u>thinking differently</u> long before all those things showed up in my life. My thinking changed and then I changed. I deliberately CHOSE the way I wanted to act. I deliberately chose the words I wanted to say. I trained myself to think the way my role models thought. And eventually, quietly, without any fanfare, I realized I had become that person.

Once I had become a professional businesswoman, it wasn't that difficult to imagine myself as a business owner. I began to model the behavior of the original founder of the company for whom I worked. The man who hired me was the kind of person who did what he thought was right and, if necessary, asked for forgiveness afterwards rather than asking permission beforehand. He believed that he was the best insurance broker his clients would ever find! His boldness in business was very different from the way I'd learned to survive in the environment where I grew up. But I watched and listened, and I began to act boldly like Fred. I began to believe that I was the best insurance agent for my clients because I truly cared about protecting them, their family, their homes, their vehicles, and their businesses. Where I had been timid about asking people if they wanted to buy their insurance from me, I boldly began to assume that they would. Many of those assumptions resulted in new clients. Those new clients translated into increased income and referrals to more new clients. The more new business I brought in, the bolder I got! In acting like Fred, I was acting like a business owner. Before long, I was one!

You can copy the best characteristics from a number of people. They don't have to be people with whom you have a personal relationship, or even any contact with. They can be teachers, historical figures, television personalities, movie stars, or other admirable people. (Be careful which celebrity you choose because many are more dysfunctional than you are.) Biographical books or movies can be great resources on people whose behaviors you may want to model, but your role models or mentors don't have to be famous or successful by the world's standards.

You can find role models for every area of life. I found guidance for day-to-day living from others. For example, while watching me load the washing machine, a friend gently said, *"Gosh, Rhonda, how many things are you going to cram into that washer?"* I hadn't grown up with a washer and dryer, and no one had ever shown me how to use a washing machine. You would think it would be common sense to know how much you could put into a washing machine and have the clothes come out clean, but it wasn't "common" for me! A modern washer and dryer were so advanced compared to the washtub and washboard, wringer washing machine, and clothesline I had grown up using. The whole process of going from dirty clothes to clean dry clothes hanging in my closet an hour later seemed almost miraculous! It hadn't occurred to me that I shouldn't cram a washing machine so full that the clothes wouldn't get clean!

Is there something you want to be better at doing? Is there something you'd like to learn how to do? Find people who did it successfully and ask them how they did it. Surprisingly, many people will give you their time and advice if they know you are genuinely trying to improve your life and that you want nothing more from them than their advice. Try looking for people on the Internet. If the person you want to model happens to be a celebrity, an athlete, or a politician, you can likely find his or her contact information in a book called *The Address Book* by Michael Levine.

I have had a lot of success in getting people to give their advice when I've written a short letter with a specific request and provided a self-addressed, stamped envelope and a blank piece of paper for them to respond to me quickly and easily. I have letters from a former President and a Vice President of the United States, federal and state Congress people, a sitting Supreme Court judge, actors, professional athletes, authors, and successful business men and women – all freely giving their advice and all because I asked for it. Don't hesitate to ask. All they can do is say "no" or ignore your request. And if they do, don't take it personally. Just move on. If they give their advice, take it, implement it, and then add your unique personality, your style, your twist to make it your own.

Before you act on anyone's advice about what job to take, who to date, how to spend your money, or anything else that will affect your life, ask yourself if the person is qualified to give you that type of advice. Consider that if you want to know how to rebuild the engine in a car, you don't ask a hairdresser. Likewise, if you want to know how to add highlights to your hair, you don't ask a mechanic. If you want to know how to make more money than you need to survive, don't ask someone who is struggling financially. There will be many people who want to try to tell you what you should do. Ask if the person has anything to gain by giving you advice. If he or she does, consider getting the opinion of someone you respect who has absolutely nothing to gain by giving you advice.

When you are in doubt about the way you should act or what you should say or do and have no appropriate mentor to ask, imagine what a wise person would do. Only fools believe only what they already know or can see. Only fools refuse to be taught by people who know more than they do about subjects of importance. Most people are not goal-oriented and on their way to success. So be careful not to model behavior from someone who is not following specific goals and living according to the principles that are proven to result in success.

FAMOUS WORLD CHANGERS

One of the people I've tried to model is Winston Churchill. He exhibited strength in the face of very frightening circumstances with many people around him putting pressure on him to "fix" circumstances that appeared to be irreparable. During World War II the enemy, Hitler, was determined to rule the world at any cost, and all of England was looking to Churchill to have all the answers. What tremendous pressure he must have faced. In the midst of all that, he said some famous words that have stuck with me since the day I read them when I was just a young girl in elementary school. He said, *"Never, never, never give up."* Bombs were dropping on his country, walls were shaking, and his people were crying over the deaths of their sons, the soldiers he had sent into battle; but he didn't give up. Ultimately, the war was won. The good guys triumphed, and evil was thwarted. I'm all about what works, and Churchill demonstrated with his life that persistence works, even in the face of seemingly impossible adversity.

Another one of my role models is Mother Theresa. Here was a woman born into a well-to-do family who could have lived a quiet life of comfort, but who chose a vow of poverty. More specifically, she chose a life of caring for people who were difficult to care for. The people she gave her life to were often dirty and dying of communicable diseases – people whom no one wanted to deal with and who were literally left to die in the streets. Although she took a vow of poverty, she successfully raised millions of dollars and built orphanages, hospitals, and schools. She was an amazing woman who put the needs of total strangers before her own needs and desires. Her life taught me that I am capable of putting up with difficult people and even helping people who are hurtful, selfish, and uncaring.

Many of the people I've modeled are people who overcame adversity and literally changed the world. They include people who invented the telephone, the electric light bulb, the personal computer, and many other inventions that changed all our lives. Some built railroads that changed our country forever; some built businesses that have employed millions of people; and some of them are real-life heroes who risked their lives to save the lives of others. But all overcame extreme difficulties.

For example, Thomas Edison, who tried thousands of times unsuccessfully to harness electricity to create light through a bulb, finally did so, and consequently changed the world. Imagine failing literally thousands of times and getting up the next day to try again.

Mr. Edison had the stamina, focus, and persistence to ignore people who likely made fun of him or talked unkindly to him or about him. I imagine that those qualities were developed when he faced adversity in his childhood. I read that when Thomas Edison was a young boy in elementary school, his teacher sent him home with a note saying that he was not mentally able to handle an education! Imagine how he must have felt with all the kids making fun of him, his family disappointed in him, and the entire town thinking he was "retarded."

Thomas Edison never did go back to school. He read and learned at home, and he moved out to live on his own at age 16. Eventually he invented the incandescent light bulb, the phonograph (record player), and the very first camera used to film movies. He had a world record of 1,093 total inventions for which he held patents at the United States Patent Office! When asked what characteristics he thought were necessary to success, Mr. Edison was said to have responded, "Common sense, hard work, and stick-to-it-iveness."

Mary Kay Ash also overcame tremendous unfairness to become one of the most successful women in America. For 25 years she had worked her way up the corporate ladder to become the national training director for her employer. Time after time she saw men whom she had trained being promoted over her and paid more than her. When one of these men was promoted and paid double her salary, she resigned from her position. She decided to write a book that would give women the specific steps they would need to achieve success, limited only by their commitment and willingness to work. As she wrote the book, she realized that she was actually creating a business plan for a company that could help hundreds of thousands of women achieve their own measure of success.

Mary Kay Ash started that company with $5,000 of her hard-earned savings. The unfairness she'd experienced motivated her to establish a company based on faith, family, and career – in that order. She was determined not to create a cut-throat competitive business model, but one where people encourage one another and celebrate each other's successes. Although she has since passed away, her company continues to thrive. According to the Mary Kay Inc. website, this company now has more than 1.7 million independent consultants. The details of how Mary Kay Ash built her amazing company are in her book, *The Mary Kay Way*.

True stories about people like Thomas Edison and Mary Kay Ash are fascinating and inspiring. If you want to read a compilation of the secrets of success of some of the United States' most influential people of the early 1900's, read Napoleon Hill's *Think and Grow Rich* or *The Law of Success*. Other advice and inspiring true stories are in books written by Earl Nightingale, Zig Ziglar, Dr. Denis Waitley, Brian Tracy, Dr. Norman Vincent Peale, Dale Carnegie, Anthony Robbins, and many others.

I have done my best to emulate never giving up from Winston Churchill, tenacity from Thomas Edison, work ethic from my high school teacher, sales from author and motivational speaker Zig Ziglar, positive thinking from Dr. Norman Vincent Peale, investing from Warren Buffett, loving people who are difficult to love from Mother Theresa, and so much more from many others, most of whom I have never met.

I hope you see from these examples that you don't have to sit in a classroom somewhere to learn how to be the person you want to be. No matter what, don't lie, cheat, steal or make any other wrong choices because if you do, the wrong choice is what you will be known for doing. And if you're known for wrong behavior, you will not be offered the advice, assistance, and opportunities that will make you real money and genuine prosperity.

CHAPTER 8

YOU'RE HERE FOR A REASON

I t doesn't matter if you didn't get the education you wanted. It doesn't matter if it seems that everyone else in the world has advantages that you don't have. Although it would have been wonderful to have a great family who loved us unconditionally, a wonderful place to live, a great education at good schools, and every other advantage we may have been lacking, what we have to focus on is **what we do have** and how best to use it to create successful lives. Bear in mind that there are people who had a decent family, received a good education, and had every other advantage we didn't, who have failed to do anything meaningful with their lives. My point is that all those advantages don't guarantee success.

On the other hand, there are many people who have had little or no formal education and innumerable disadvantages, but who marshaled their determination, natural intelligence, ambition, willingness to learn, and desire to succeed and made a success of their lives. Books are full of the stories of people like this. YOU can be one of them! You may already be one of them. You don't have to be the next Bill Gates and invent a new computer operating system, or be a talented athlete, a famous musician, or a well-known actor to be a successful person.

You can be someone who cleans the toilets in a factory and grows up to be the president of your own company. Sound unrealistic? That is my friend's story. He went from being a teenager cleaning the bathrooms at a factory, to being the chauffeur to a CEO, to starting his own company, which has grown to be one of the largest companies of its kind in his state. He accomplished all of this without a college education. I'm not advocating against a good education. But I have to point out that lacking the advantage of a traditional education doesn't disqualify you from the race to success.

Give yourself credit for the life education you did get. As long as you are still breathing, you are still in the game! **What you do** with what education you have gained through school, reading on your own, skills learned on the job, and the lessons learned from all of the experiences of your life is what REALLY counts.

We've learned numerous skills, some even before we were verbal. While many of the survival skills we learned in dysfunctional environments have to be polished or replaced by skills more appropriate to our current lives, everything we did to survive adversity has built in us a strength that others simply do not have. Start with who you are as a result of what has happened to you. While it is true that the bad decisions of others have left many of us scarred, we also have a lot of positive traits that we tend to discount or overlook entirely.

By learning to see yourself as the strong, capable, controlled, powerful, confident, educated person that you are, you can quit seeing what you're not and begin appreciating who you are. Talking to yourself and seeing yourself in a positive way is not just fluff designed to make you feel good. I'm talking about putting a meaningful value on the fact that people who survive tragedy, trauma, or dysfunction can deal with what would devastate most people.

What if our life's purpose is to accomplish an assignment too difficult for others to handle? Consider the following:

- You may know how to "read a situation" and know when trouble is about to break out better than most people. That skill can prove to be tremendously valuable in a customer service setting, sales, law enforcement, or a combat situation as a soldier.

- You may be adept at telling a joke or lightening the mood and distracting people who are "heating up." This is another very good skill that can be helpful in dealing with neighbors, co-workers, or customers in any situation where keeping the peace is important. In other words, this skill has almost universal appeal.

- You may be an excellent communicator or a natural peacemaker who is able to get people to come together and see each other's side of things. If you were the child who always tried to make everything okay, you are probably excellent at dealing with difficult customers or helping to resolve conflict between co-workers.

- You may be able to deal with a child with difficult behaviors because you were like that child and understand what he or she has been through better than anyone else can. You may be the only one able to really reach that child.

- You have talents you haven't yet discovered.

- You have talents you know about but haven't yet used.

- You have resources and prospective mentors you haven't yet fully tapped.

- You are not out of ideas.

Just because no one has recognized your positive qualities yet doesn't mean they are not there. Sometimes we have to let people know we are good and why we are good. There's nothing wrong with being your own best advocate.

If you've experienced unfairness, tragedy, or abuse, you may have a fire inside of you looking for a positive release in your life. When you figure out what you are uniquely suited to do, it won't feel like work. Don't discount as unimportant the qualities that come easily to you.

At times it may feel like you are worn out, but you CAN dig deep and pull out of your circumstances some more. You are NOT out of the fight until you decide to give up and give in. Resist the temptation to do this. It is your call, though. No one is going to fight for you if you won't do it for yourself.

I spent the first thirty years of my life wondering why I'd been born and how my life might have been different had I come from a loving family that wanted me, nurtured me, and encouraged me. I thought many times about the two kids who were chosen by the people who came to interview me for adoption when I was 7. Years later, I heard that the boy who was adopted became the general manager of a world-renowned hotel in New York and the girl became a neurosurgeon. I wondered what wonderful, high-powered career I'd have now if I'd had the benefit of all the education I'd wanted, paid for by a family who told me that my sole job in life was to be a student.

One casual conversation with a friend began to change the way I looked at my life. My friend, who came from a loving family, told me she admired my willingness to leave my stable job and step out into my own business. She told me how she thought I was brave and seemed to be driven by some determination to succeed that she just didn't have. She didn't envy me and didn't want what I had or the life I was living, but she was simply observing that she didn't have the ambition and drive it would take to work sixty or more hours every week and to deal with the challenges that went along with the decision to start my own business and make it successful.

In one short conversation, this friend moved me from thinking that if I had been raised in a loving family, I would have accomplished so much more, to beginning to understand that it's likely that I would not have accomplished nearly as much had I not had a fire in my belly that came from the need to prove my worthiness.

I began to understand that the "bad" things that had happened to me were the very things that prepared me for the work I was doing. For example, had we not lost what little we had in a fire due to lack of insurance when I was 8 years old, I wouldn't have thought the concept of insurance was so amazing, and I probably wouldn't have been as passionate about protecting people with appropriate insurance coverage.

Had I not had the experience of having nothing and being hungry, perhaps I wouldn't have been so willing to take the leap and open my own business. I figured that I'd been hungry before and worked my way into a good job with good benefits. I knew that if this business didn't make it, I could work my way up to a good salary and benefits again.

Had I not taken that leap of faith and opened my own business, I never would have helped pave the way for a change in rating insurance premiums for homes for abused children that has resulted in millions of dollars in savings annually. I wouldn't have influenced the way insurance companies now look at insuring child welfare organizations. And I wouldn't have advocated for a change in workers' compensation insurance that has saved millions of dollars of premiums for foster family agencies.

Yes, there were times when it was very difficult. There was a lot of disappointment and very hard work. But the fear of failure and the desire to eat and to sleep in a safe, warm bed at night were powerful motivations. I'm confident that I have done what I was able to do BECAUSE OF rather than IN SPITE OF what happened to me as a child. And I'm not the only one who believes this to be true.

In their book, *Cradles of Eminence*, researchers Victor and Mildred Goertzel reviewed the childhood family life of 700 of the world's most successful people. Their goal was to identify the early experiences that contributed to their remarkable achievements.

All of their "research subjects" are widely known for their personal accomplishments. Their names are easily recognizable: Franklin D. Roosevelt, Helen Keller, Winston Churchill, Albert Schweitzer, Gandhi, Albert Einstein, Sigmund Freud, and many more. What they discovered was fascinating!

Many of these successful people came from deeply troubled childhoods. They had endured extreme poverty, broken homes, and abuse. Many had to deal with very serious physical handicaps, such as deafness, blindness, or crippled limbs. Interestingly, most of those who became successful writers and playwrights had watched their own parents struggle with intense psychological dramas. The researchers concluded that the drive to compensate for their disadvantages actually drove these people straight into the arms of outrageous personal achievement!

Can you believe that there is a purpose in your pain? I found my purpose, and when I did, my self-esteem and dignity came along with it. If you don't find the purpose of your suffering, you could develop a victim mentality. When you feel like a victim of people or circumstances that are out of your control, you won't take opportunities that come your way. You won't take calculated risks to move forward in your life and career. And consequently, you'll miss out on a lot of what this life has to offer. Perhaps more importantly, you'll miss out on doing what you were born to do.

Everything that you've experienced in your life has made you the person you are and prepared you for your unique purpose. You have been created and prepared for something. You MUST find out what it is and go for it with all you've got. There is a purpose to your life, and when you find it, you will excel at it, money will

Everyone has the ability to do something well – even at a genius level. Your job is to figure out what it is.

follow, good relationships will be developed, and you will be in better circumstances than you could have thought possible. If you haven't experienced financial prosperity, great relationships, and fulfillment, it might be that you haven't yet found your purpose.

It doesn't matter how old you are or how many times you've tried. You can try one more time. You can spend the next year figuring out your purpose and your natural talents, or you can spend the next year doing what you've always done. Either way, at the end of the year you'll be a year older! You might as well determine to devote the time necessary to finding your unique purpose, the reason you were born.

You ARE here for a reason. It's your responsibility to find out what it is and go after it with everything you've got.

WHO ARE YOU?

We are happy to the extent that we are in control of our lives, that we are doing what we're good at, that we feel appreciated and valued, that we have good relationships with quality people, and

SUCCEED BECAUSE OF WHAT YOU'VE BEEN THROUGH

that we are financially self-sufficient. The question is how to figure out what we should be doing so that we'll have *all* of these things. This can be difficult, but it's not impossible to figure out.

To identify your purpose and the unique set of talents, skills, and abilities that have been planted inside of you, consider the answers to the following questions. Your answers will reveal some of the clues to discovering your purpose and the "assignment" you are uniquely qualified to accomplish.

1. What are the qualities that you like best about your personality?

2. What comes easily to you? What do you do well?

3. What do you know something about? What do you know more about than the average person?

4. What bugs you? What can you do to change it?

5. What are you interested in?

6. What opinions and judgments do you have that influence your decisions, actions and thoughts?

7. What would you do if you weren't afraid?

8. Is there something you would do if you knew you couldn't fail?

9. What do people come to you for? *(To get advice, to listen to their problems, to get a laugh, to do them a favor?)*

10. What compliments did you receive as a child? An adolescent? Now?

11. What is the result of your creativity?

12. What makes you laugh?

13. What are your favorite talents, skills, or abilities?

14. What were your nicknames as a child? An adolescent? Now? (positive or demeaning)

15. What should your nickname be now? (positive only)

16. What are your daydreams?

17. What heroic feats have you performed?

18. What quality have you most improved since becoming an adult?

19. What things come out of your mouth on a regular basis? (What are you known for saying? What would you like to be known for saying? These are clues to what you "stand for.")

20. List all the reasons you should congratulate yourself.

21. What is the funniest joke you've ever told or the best practical joke you've ever pulled?

22. If you had to summarize your life into a motto or slogan, what would it be? (*This may be the same as what you'd like to shout out loud to friends, family, co-workers, and everyone else you meet. These are more clues to what you "stand for.")*

23. List the warnings/advice you heard as a child.

24. List the character traits or actions that helped you through the tough times in your life.

25. What advice would you give to a young person who will be 21 years old?

26. What's your best advice to a person getting married?

27. What advice would you give to someone about to have his or her first child?

28. What advice would you give to the parent of a child with health or behavioral difficulties?

29. What advice would you give to someone opening his or her own business?

30. What advice would you give to someone with a terminal illness?

31. What do you know for sure? (*How is it different from what you knew when you were younger? How do you think it might be different 25 years from now?*)

32. List the things you want to do before you die. (*If you're bold, set timelines on each of these.*)

33. List the most exhilarating experiences you have had.

34. List the places, people, and things you've seen that altered your view of the world.

35. What were the difficult experiences of your life, and what lessons did you learn from them?

36. List the beliefs you'd go out on a limb for.

37. List the people you would step in front of a bullet to protect.

38. What were the biggest turning points in your life?

39. How have you sabotaged yourself? (*Or how do you hold yourself back from what you really want?*)

40. What people have changed your life for the better? How?

41. What positive contributions have you made in this world?

42. What words (from what person) do you long to hear?

43. Is there someone longing to hear something from you? If so, what is it and what's holding you back from saying it?

44. What traits do you value in your friends?

45. What inspires you to keep going when you get discouraged?

46. What do you want your obituary to say?

47. What miracles do you know have happened?

48. What things in nature remind you of your connection to the "big picture"?

49. What's wrong with most people nowadays?

50. If you suddenly received 10 million dollars and were told you must spend it to help others, how would you spend it?

As you review the answers to these questions, who you *really* are will begin to emerge. Once you see "the real you," you'll begin to have a sense of how valuable you truly are. The best part about this whole exercise is that your purpose, or what I call "your assignment," will begin to become evident to you.

The way we can have all the things we want in life is to find a way to live in the specific purpose for which we were uniquely created. A **big clue** to what you're supposed to do is that it will always have to do with helping others.

*Thoughts + words + actions
+ courage* x *belief* = SUCCESS

Think about how you can use your unique combination of skills, talents, abilities, personality traits, character traits, and good and bad experiences for the benefit of others. All these things, along with the things that bother you, the things that others have done *for* you, the things that have been done *to* you, the things that you have accomplished, and everything else that you've identified about yourself, uniquely qualify you for your specific purpose. Your purpose involves helping others.

Think about what people want, what they need, and what problems need to be solved. Then think about how to get what you need by solving the problems you identify.

One modern day example of someone finding a purpose and creating wealth by solving a common problem is found in the true story of Sara Blakely. According to an interview she gave on the cable television show, *The Big Idea*, she was a young woman who hated panty lines and didn't like thong underwear. She didn't want to wear pantyhose, so she thought about ideas for solving her problem. She came up with the idea of cutting the legs off a pair of pantyhose and wearing the top part under her slacks. She experimented with sewing the bottom of the leg portion that had been cut off until they no longer rolled up. The results are what we now know as Spanx, which are now sold all over the United States. By using her creativity, acting on it, having the courage to contact a buyer for a major department store, and believing in herself and her product, Sara Blakely solved a problem for herself and for millions of women across the country. The same combination of creative thoughts, positive words, action, courage and belief will work for anyone who applies them.

When you use *who you are* to help others, you are simultaneously helping yourself! How can you make *who you are* generate revenue for you? Some ideas are as follows:

- Identify a problem people have and figure out how you can provide a solution in the form of a product or helpful service.

- Identify something that people need or want and figure out how you can provide it.

- Teach others what you are able to do well. You can do this by writing a blog, giving seminars, or doing workshops in your area of expertise. You don't have to be a credentialed teacher to teach people. For example, if you happen to be good with electronics, such as computers and cell phones, you could work as a sales person in a store that sells these products. By helping people understand how electronics can help them save time, make money, and get organized, you'll be an effective sales person. The best sales people effectively communicate how the client will benefit from the product or service. In other words, they focus on the client's needs and wants rather than on the product, its manufacturer, the salesperson, or anything else.

You may not even realize what you're naturally good at doing. When something comes easily to us, we have a tendency to think it comes easily to everyone. We tend to discount our natural talents. For example, are you more patient with customers than your co-workers? Do you easily remember numbers and details that others have to write down? Can you easily do something that others find difficult to accomplish?

When you find the thing that you do really well, you'll enjoy doing it and it won't be a hassle for you at all. The right work won't even feel like work! That's why we must not dismiss the possibility of a specific job or line of work because someone else told you it's too hard or too much of a hassle. It may be a hassle for them because they're not cut out for it. You may be able to easily do something someone else isn't able to do.

Root out the obstacles that will keep you from taking this information and doing something with it. Focus on the things that cause you to use this information to achieve your goals.

- What keeps you from moving toward your goals? Fear of failure? Your beliefs about business owners, success, money? Fear of success? What you will have to give up in order to pay the price to reach your goal?

- What would cause you to move toward your goals? Desire? The revenge of success? The drive to prove yourself? Fear of feeling regret later for not having tried?

- What do you need?

  • Support
  • Help with responsibilities

- Education
- Mentors in areas of inexperience or weakness
- A plan
- Positive, productive relationships

  - What activities do you need to eliminate that are not part of your future?

CREATED TO BE CREATIVE

You may be wondering how to "connect the dots" between who you are and how to use that information to reach your goals. Consider that from the first time young children draw something or make something for Mommy or Daddy, it's easy to see how pleased they are with themselves when they create something and how important the approval of the recipient of the gift is to them. People create. That's what we do. We were born to create. But for those of us who grew up in dysfunctional environments or experienced unfairness or tragedy, the creativity in us gets quashed and sometimes completely destroyed. We get scolded (or worse) for making a mess, for getting dirty, or for breaking something – then we withdraw.

When we hear comments, such as *"You're stupid, an idiot; you'll never amount to anything; you're just like your father [mother]"* – fill in the blank with whatever "loser" you're being compared to – we withdraw further. Sometimes we withdraw so much so that the sparkle that was once in our little eyes isn't even a glowing ember anymore... until... a teacher, social worker, neighbor, friend, relative, co-worker, or spouse says or does something to reignite that spark.

You may be thinking, *"That's not me. I wasn't physically abused."* To an extent, this withdrawal happens to all of us when we are corrected. Even in a loving family, being told *"no," "don't do that,"* or *"bad boy or girl"* can result in suppressed creativity, even though it is often necessary for a proper understanding of right and wrong. But when attempts at correction are made in anger, are made in the presence of instability, or are inconsistent, the results can be as damaging as physical abuse.

For example, if you do something one day and it is okay, but you do the exact same thing a different day and you are in trouble for it, you don't know how to make corrections in your behavior to prevent getting in trouble again. When you don't know what's going to trigger the anger of a person who has authority over you, you wind up either overcompensating by walking on eggshells and trying to be perfect, which sets you up to fail over and over again because it's impossible to be perfect, or you quit caring and don't try at all.

Inside of any seed is the power to create the thing that created the seed.

If your natural creativity has been damaged or inhibited, I have good news! It's not gone. It's just buried, like a seed in soil that needs sun, water, and nutrients to grow into a strong, fruit-bearing tree.

Think about that. Every tomato seed has the potential to become a vine, leaves, flowers, and tomatoes, many tomatoes. Every watermelon seed has the potential within it to become a vine, leaves, and multiple watermelons. And so on.

Each of us has the seed of something great in us. It is the seed of the thing that can make us so much more than what we are. We have the ability to make our idea a reality. In order to activate it, we have to retrain ourselves to think with the kind of creativity that comes naturally to little children. This is the creativity that is accompanied by belief that what we're thinking about can become a reality.

No one who knew me as a teenager or young adult could have guessed what I was capable of and what I would do with my life. YOU are capable of much more than it may appear. YOU are the only one who can activate your brain to think, to speak, and to do what will lead you to your success in every area of your life.

If you doubt that you are creative or think your natural creativity has been irreparably damaged, remember that the capacity of our minds to create, imagine, and communicate is beyond the understanding of even the greatest physicians, scientists, and researchers in the world. Consider also that our abilities to imagine and communicate are the things that truly set us apart from every other species on Earth.

Our ability to think is the seed of our wealth.
Your mind will come up with ideas to
make money for you.

Unlike any other animal, we are the only species with a mind that can think, imagine, dream and create, and then effectively communicate to others our thoughts, dreams, and abstract concepts. We have the ability to come up with ideas for solving problems, creating new products, writing music, providing needed services, discovering cures for diseases, and much, much more. This is not by accident. We were designed to be creative. If we see what we want clearly and vividly in our imagination, often we can bring that vision to pass in our lives by the words we speak, the choices we make, our behaviors, and our persistence. Eventually we can turn our thoughts into reality.

The most complicated and intricate, yet least understood, computer ever created is in the shell sitting on top of your neck. It is the human brain. The brain can conceive, believe, and influence the reality of amazing inventions, cures, vaccines, symphonies, art, buildings, equipment, etc. The brain lets us know if we are in danger and what to do about it. It gives us what we call intuition and discernment. Our brain allows us to access the gifts, talents, and abilities that are exactly what are needed to make the dreams in our hearts and the solutions to things that bother us become realities. We are capable of much more than we think and much more than is apparent.

Every creation and invention of man that we enjoy today was first an idea in someone's mind, from the chair you are sitting in to

We earn more money with our
brains than with our bodies.

the cell phone you communicate with. Then it was vividly described with words before the idea actually became a reality. Many of the things we now use every day sounded like science fiction when their inventors first spoke about them. You could say that the ideas and the words were the seeds that ultimately grew into every invented and created thing.

Generally speaking, physical work pays less than being paid to think and communicate. The more you think and effectively communicate, the more money you'll make. For example, a physicist is paid to think but a person hired to dig ditches is paid to use his or her arms, legs, and back. The physicist earns much more than the person who does physical labor. The architect earns more than the construction worker.

All honest work is noble, and one job is not better than another. The point I'm making is that regardless of what you do for work, THINK! How can it be done better? Faster? Less expensively? More efficiently? What problem exists that you have a solution for? That solution might lead to the product or service which results in your financial prosperity. Even if your boss isn't interested in your ideas, someone will be. Write them down. Keep a notebook or file of all your ideas. You might find that one of those ideas will become your ticket to the life you want to live.

The root of all commerce is providing a product or service people need or want. When you figure out how to meet a need or want and find a way to deliver it, you will earn a living, and perhaps even enough to hire employees to help you deliver the product or service. Or you may sell your idea to a company that has the resources to make it a reality without you ever having to invest the time and money into building your own business.

There is no other person on earth who has the exact same combination of personality and character traits that you have.

How do you come up with your "million-dollar idea"? *Pay attention to people's problems.* If you can come up with a solution to a problem that people commonly have, your solution can have universal appeal. The broader the appeal, the larger the number of people who will buy your product or service. The more people there are who will buy what you are selling, the more income you'll generate.

Don't compare yourself to anyone. Your set of skills, talents, abilities, and experiences are different from everyone else's. Just like the seed of a tomato plant contains everything it needs to become the roots, the plant, the leaves, and the tomatoes, you have everything inside you to become what YOU were designed to be. The person next to you has a completely different set of skills, talents, and abilities to accomplish a different assignment, *their assignment*. What works for them may not work for you. One person's skill set or assignment is not better or worth more than another. They're just different.

Think of it this way, Kobe Bryant is one of the best basketball players in the world, but he may not be able to play golf as well as Tiger Woods. Should he feel bad if he can't play golf as well as one of the greatest golfers in the world? Of course not. We can be happy for the talents and accomplishments of others without it being a reflection of or a judgment on what we are able to do. To compare ourselves to others does nothing but create unnecessary stress and pressure in our lives. Don't do it to yourself, and don't allow others to do it to you.

Hopefully by now you have gained a better understanding of why you have done what you've done, forgiven those who hurt you, chosen your role models and mentors, and seen a glimpse of who you really are and what your unique purpose is. Now you are thinking differently than you have before.

CHAPTER 9

MAKING RIGHT CHOICES AND TREATING PEOPLE RIGHT

I 've mentioned making right choices and treating people
right, so before we go to the next level of our purpose, let's
spend a little time defining specifically what that means.

WHAT IT MEANS TO MAKE RIGHT CHOICES

It's important to note that those of us who came from
dysfunctional or abusive backgrounds may not have the "automatic
moral compass" that people from a stable upbringing often have.
What was considered "right" by the people who raised us is often
distorted at best and downright criminal at worst. So, it can be
somewhat more difficult for us to make right choices because this
often does not come naturally for us. We either don't have an
automatic barometer of right and wrong, or the one we have is
distorted by the actions of those who raised us.

Therefore, when we are unsure of what to do, we have to check
our choices against those of the person we want to be, against the
characteristics necessary for success, and against decisions that

we think our role models would make. If they don't match up, we shouldn't make that choice. This means, among other things, never, ever do anything illegal, unethical, or immoral. Even when something is legal, it may still be immoral. If you have to wonder, *"Is this the right thing to do?"* it's probably not.

Once you've decided what kind of person you want to be, decide never to do or say anything that isn't in keeping with what that person would do. When a situation comes up that involves something that the "new you" wouldn't do, the answer to the question of whether or not you'll do it will be obvious. The answer is NO – period.

Just because you can,
doesn't mean you should!

To make my point on this in an exaggerated way, if your buddies are all going to steal a car and you don't know if you should go with them, ask yourself if your role model would do it, if it's going to move you closer to your goals or away from them, and if it matches with your list of characteristics of successful people. (*If you think your role model would do something illegal, unethical, or immoral, you've chosen the wrong role model!*)

Checking to see if a decision moves you closer to your goals and lines up with the person you want to be will get easier with each decision that you make. Every right decision straightens your automatic moral compass until, ultimately, making right choices becomes natural and effortless.

TREATING PEOPLE RIGHT

Treating people right means treating people with the character traits of truly successful people; e.g., integrity, honesty, loyalty, courtesy, and kindness. Genuinely caring about people and expressing that care in small but meaningful ways is one of the keys to getting all you want. It may appear to you to be completely disconnected; trust me, it's not. This may sound manipulative, but if you treat people properly for the sake of being the person you want to be, and not for what they might be able to do for you, there's nothing manipulative about your words or actions. For example, if you smile at people and make eye contact when you say, *"Thank you,"* if you ask how people are and really want to know the answer, if you take the time to give an encouraging word to people, benefits will come back to you in ways you may not be able to imagine now.

Remember that you never know what others are going through. The clerk behind the counter may have just lost her mother. The waitress may be facing eviction because her roommate moved out without paying her half of the rent. The bank teller's husband might have stayed out all night, or the receptionist's teenager might be stealing what little money she has to buy drugs. These types of things are going on all around us. You may be thinking, *"I've got my own problems. I don't have any time or energy to worry about the problems of others."* That may be true, but it costs nothing and requires very little effort to treat people with kindness, keeping in mind that you're not the only one facing challenges.

When we look at others with kind eyes, smile at them, speak with a calm tone of voice, and touch them gently and appropriately, they feel respected, valued, and worthy of good things. When people feel valued, they are more likely to treat you the same way. So, make an intentional effort to look people in the eyes when they're speaking to you or if you're talking to them. If they don't reciprocate, don't worry about it. Continue to do what you know is right regardless of what other people do. As is evident all around us, not everyone treats people right. Not everyone is willing to make the efforts necessary to achieve true success.

An essential part of developing good relationships is to take a deep breath and intentionally change your tone of voice BEFORE you do or say anything hurtful, in anger, or with frustration. *This is especially true if you're speaking to a child.*

NEVER act arrogantly, lie, cheat, or steal. Don't tell anyone else something told to you in confidence. Do not talk about others behind their backs, even if what you want to say is true. Be the

---

It's important that you make right choices and treat people right, especially when you don't feel like it. When you least feel like doing the right thing is when it will benefit you most.

---

kind of person people can trust. Listen, learn, and implement good advice from successful people who try to help you. Don't ever intentionally hurt anyone physically, verbally, or emotionally. If you find out that something you say or do does hurt someone, tell him or her that you're sorry and that you will try not to do it again. It can be difficult to say you're sorry, but the benefits of saying these little words are huge.

Will people always do the same for you? No. Will some of them take advantage of you? Yes. But when someone begins to take advantage of you, distance yourself from them.

There are rewards for doing what is right and there are consequences for doing what is wrong and failing to do what is right. To illustrate what I mean by choosing to treat people right, consider this scenario:

You finally have a decent car, a car you can call your own. You're driving down the road to pick up your date and some careless person slams into the back of your new car. You and the other driver pull your cars over to the side of the road, and you jump out screaming at this guy for not paying attention and for ruining your car. He yells back at you; and without even thinking, you take a swing at the guy. The police show up, the guy presses charges, and you get booked. Let's say it's Friday afternoon and the judge won't hear the case until Monday morning.

You're locked up for the weekend. Your boss told you last week that if you missed one more day of work, you'd be fired. The person you're dating told you that if you were late one more time, it was over. You have no money for bail and know no one who does. So there you sit in jail with your car impounded and the daily charges for impounding your car adding up. You're wondering how you're going to come up with the money for bail and the money to get your car back since you know that you'll lose your job. All of this happened because of a split-second decision to hit someone – NOT because of bad luck or the other guy being a jerk. No, YOU ARE RESPONSIBLE for this mess!

Now imagine another scenario:

Picture the same circumstance with the same careless person hitting your car, only this time you take a deep breath before you get out of the car. You walk back to meet the person who did this, and you wait to hear what he or she has to say. That person gets out of the car and says, "I'm sorry; it was an accident." (Even if he or she gets out of the car angry, you just say, "Let's let the police decide who's at fault.") You know

179

that getting angry and yelling and calling this person names isn't going to fix your car, so you calmly take down his or her information, file a police report, and go on your way. You aren't late for that night's date. You still have a job. You don't spend the weekend in jail, or spend your money to get your car out of impound, or have to hire a lawyer to get you out on bail. And instead of your date being angry at you, he or she is sympathetic over what you had to go through!

Hopefully, these illustrations help you understand the importance of making the decision to treat people right in every situation regardless of your feelings. Making bad decisions can cost you money, time, and your reputation; making good decisions ultimately results in you earning more money, having better relationships, and feeling more peace in your life.

Treating other people properly, regardless of how they treat you or what they may be able to do for you or to you, shows that you have a level of class that sets you apart from most people. Being good and doing good for other people plants seeds of goodness that are guaranteed to come back to you in some way. You've probably heard the phrase, *"What goes around comes around."* It's so true.

For example, if you stop to help someone who's broken down in the middle of the road, give someone a ride, help someone carry a heavy load to his or her car, or stay late to finish something that is needed at work, somehow, someway, from someone (maybe not from the person for whom you did the favor), you will be paid back. You may not be able to see how doing these things could possibly benefit you, but trust me; doing something for someone else WILL ALWAYS come back to you in some good way. It may not be money, but it might be something that is far more important than that.

CHAPTER 10

SERVING OTHERS IS THE KEY

Regardless of whether you hate your job, can't stand your boss, are ridiculed by your coworkers, are treated harshly by customers, or generally are mistreated, if your employer is paying you, you must do the best job you can for the time you have sold to your employer. That's right, I said *"the time you sold."* The fact is that you are self-employed. In reality, everyone is self-employed. We all get 24 hours every day. When you take a job, you are literally selling your time to your employer. Once you've sold that time, your employer "owns you" for those hours. So during those hours, you must do whatever your employer wants you to do, so long as it's legal and ethical. In other words, if the boss wants you to scrub the toilets, you should do it, and what's more, do it better than anyone ever has. If you're not adding to the profitability and efficiency of the company, why should they employ you? If you were an employer, you wouldn't pay employees who didn't do what you were paying them to do.

While you're doing what you're being paid to do, maintain a good attitude. Don't grumble or complain. Even if you're thinking negative thoughts, keep them to yourself and *act* as though you have a good attitude. The emphasis here is clearly on the word *act*. If you don't genuinely feel it, act as though you have a good attitude. The most educated, most skilled, most talented employee will miss opportunities for advancement if he or she has a bad attitude. Skill never justifies negativity in the long run. The employer may need the skill for a period of time, but will eventually replace the talented employees who fail to improve their attitude. More on how to adopt and maintain a positive attitude later.

Do not rely solely on your job description: Do what needs to be done. If you're done with what you've been assigned to do, ask for more work or look around and do what you see that needs to be done. Ask your co-workers and boss what you can do for them. If they have nothing more for you to do, read up on the company's products and services, the industry, and whatever other information you can find that will make you a more valuable employee. Do not play on the Internet, make personal phone calls, read a book, or any of the other things people do that contribute nothing of value to the company. Doing things at work that don't benefit the company indicates to your employer that there isn't enough work to justify your position.

There is no such thing as job security. The day of getting a job, staying on that job for thirty years, retiring, and then receiving the majority of your paycheck and health insurance for the rest of your life is long gone. Many have thought that they had that arrangement, only to find that the company they worked for went out of business or the people responsible for their retirement benefits mismanaged or embezzled from the retirement fund, leaving nothing to be paid out. The way to avoid this fate is to not trust your future to anyone but yourself. Accept responsibility for your own employment, benefits, and retirement.

The only real job security is in being the very best YOU that you can be, and in so doing earning a reputation for being of service to clients, co-workers, supervisors, and vendors, regardless of how different they may be from you, how old they are, what their job is, or what your opinion of them may be. You never know where your next opportunity is going to come from. It may come from a customer impressed with the way you've handled his or her order, a supplier, or anyone else that you come in contact with in the course of your work. Opportunity may come from a coworker, or someone that a coworker knows, who leaves to open his or her own business or moves on to a different employer who is looking to hire additional help.

WORKING IN A DIFFICULT ENVIRONMENT

Many people have no choice but to work in a difficult or downright hostile environment. If you find yourself in a difficult situation, be careful not to let the negative environment or hostile people influence your words and actions. You will sabotage your potential success if you let a bad atmosphere get inside of you.

Letting the negativity of others make you negative is like water flooding a ship. As long as the water remains outside of the ship, the ship functions as designed. It can float above the water, plow through the water, and be surrounded by the water. But, if water begins to get inside the ship, the water will destroy the ship and everything in it.

You might think there is no way to keep negativity that's all around you from getting inside you, but it is possible to stay focused on being the person you want to be. How? Consider that if you take a cell phone and put it in a sealed plastic bag, you can drop it into a bucket of water without the cell phone being damaged at all. The water is over, under, and all around the cell phone, but it's not inside the phone because the phone is sealed.

You can protect yourself from negativity in much the same way as you protect a cell phone from water. Before going into a place that you expect will be negative or before you spend time with people you expect will have a bad attitude or be hostile toward you, take a moment to imagine a protective covering around yourself before you enter. I am aware of how silly this sounds, but you'll be amazed at how well this works! It's effective because it gives you the perspective that you are not a part of what you are entering, but rather an observer only. An observer does not assume the attitude and behaviors of those being observed. Imagine going to the zoo and observing the behaviors of the baboons. You don't come away having incorporated baboon sounds and behaviors into your life! While at the zoo (*or in a hostile work environment*), notice the similarities and differences between yourself and others, but remain clear on the fact that you are different from the objects of your observation.

Another way to keep a bad work environment from affecting you is to maintain friendships with people who have nothing to do with your workplace. Make plans and do things with friends outside of work so that work is not your sole or primary focus. If you let work become the sole source of your income, friendships, social life, affirmation, and everything else, imagine how you would feel if you lost your job. You lose everything, at least temporarily. You can always find another job, more friends, and rebuild your social life, but life's a whole lot easier if you only have to replace one aspect of your life rather than all of it at once.

To maintain your perspective, remind yourself often of your personal dreams, desires, and goals, as well as your special talents, gifts, and abilities, so that when people at work are mean, rude, jealous, or show some other negative emotion, you can think about who you really are and where you are going.

CREATE A POSITIVE ENVIRONMENT

While it may seem like you aren't important enough or advanced enough in the company to make a change, the truth is that you can be the person who changes the environment or the dynamics in your company. If you will avoid complaining, stop expecting appreciation, and show genuine concern for others (especially for the most difficult people on your job), you will be a breath of fresh air in your workplace. Why go to all that effort? Because either your boss, your future boss, or your future business partners will notice that you're different. As long as what your employer asks you to do is legal and ethical, regardless of what it is, do the work without complaint and with a smile on your face.

Look for opportunities to make positive changes at your job. Rather than being in the group that talks about problems, be the one who is known for thinking of possible solutions. For example, if people are complaining about something at work that you have a possible solution for, share your ideas with your supervisor. If it's something you can just do that needs no authorization, do it. Do not get upset if you make a suggestion that your boss doesn't implement. It could be that there's more to the situation than what you know at this time. It could mean that your suggestion is the perfect solution, but the timing just isn't right. Regardless of the reason why your idea isn't implemented, write down your suggestion, date it, and keep it somewhere so that if something ever comes up about the problem later, you can refer back to the suggestion you made on that date.

Do not complain or speak negatively about your boss or the

company. In fact, do not say anything negative to or about anyone, including a co-worker, customer, vendor, or anyone else. It's so easy to get sucked up into a negative conversation as co-workers sit at lunch or on their break and bad-mouth the boss or the company. No matter how tempting this may be and how rotten and unfair the boss and the company may be, DON'T DO IT. The only people who want to complain and hear your complaints are people who have nothing more important in their lives but gossiping and listening to the gossip of others. Don't get involved. Don't even stick around to hear it. The pain of being alone is short-term, but if you stick around and listen to others talk trash, you'll never be the person you want to be and have the life you want to have.

> *Think good things. Speak good things.*
> *Hear good things.*

If you have a valid complaint or have to report something of a negative nature, do so only to the person who can do something about it, and in a factual way, without your opinions. People who can do something about your complaint typically don't have the time to hear someone go on and on. What they do want to hear are the facts, any suggestions for resolution of the issue, and a willingness to help improve the situation. Once you have brought the issue to the attention of your supervisor, don't continue to talk to co-workers about it. There is no upside to complaining, but there is tremendous potential for downside.

For example, if you talk trash about a supervisor and the person you were talking to tells someone else who tells the supervisor, now you're not likely to be considered for a raise or promotion, and you may even be in jeopardy of losing your job. You may think that the people to whom you're talking to would never repeat what you said. But if they are willing to listen to your negative talk about something or someone, chances are that they are not above passing on what they have heard. Also, there are many little electronic gadgets that can take pictures and/or record your conversation without you even knowing it. That conversation you thought was private can be digitally transmitted to everyone you've ever met within minutes. So, don't say or do anything that you wouldn't want posted on the Internet!

Share personal problems and goals ONLY with people you can trust–people who have no ulterior motive or personal investment in the outcome of the situation other than your well-being.

Complaining, whether on the job or at home, tells people around us that we are not happy with our circumstances. The only person responsible for your happiness is YOU. Others may be concerned about you, but they can't fix the problems in your life. They can't make you happy or change your circumstances. When the co-workers, neighbors, and friends to whom you have complained go home, they turn their attention back to their own health, family, job, bills, traffic, etc., and you're left alone with your thoughts, your circumstances, your beliefs, and your choices. There's no one responsible for the outcomes in your life and no one at fault for what happens in your future but YOU. I'm not saying you shouldn't talk to anyone, but carefully choose people who can help you or encourage you and DON'T talk just to complain – especially on the job. Nothing is accomplished by that. For example, if you're having a problem with your spouse, your kids, or some other personal issue, don't talk to people on the job about it. The truth is that the problem can get worse if the people you confide in tell your business to others, or worse, use your confidential information to manipulate you to get something they want, such as ruining your marriage in order to date your spouse. Especially on the job, it's important to keep a smile on your face, have a good attitude, and keep your personal issues to yourself.

There are times when you should offer an explanation; for example, if you're unavoidably late or you missed a deadline. When you explain your situation to your supervisors, be careful not to deviate from explaining to complaining. The best way to handle any situation where you feel like you want to explain yourself is to apologize immediately, say it was unavoidable, and say that you'll do your best to make sure it never happens again. Then offer your explanation if they have time and want to hear it. Be aware of other people's time constraints. Timing is important. For example, if you come in late for work, don't burst into your boss's office and start running at the mouth about all the reasons why you're late. Your boss may be in the middle of something, and listening to you will make him or her further behind. Remember, reasons often sound like excuses, and no one wants to hear excuses.

WHAT TO EXPECT FROM YOUR JOB

Do not go to work expecting anything more than your paycheck. Do not expect appreciation or encouragement from your boss, co-workers, customers, the company's vendors, or anyone else. If it happens, consider it nice and extra, but not necessary to your happiness and fulfillment. If you EXPECT the appreciation of others, you'll usually find yourself disappointed. Do your work for the one thing your employer owes you – a paycheck at the amount agreed upon. If your employers have to take the time to tell you constantly how good a job you're doing, they could probably just do the job themselves and save the money being paid to you to do it. If you are constantly requiring affirmation that you're doing well or that you're a good person, you're lacking something in your life and expecting the job to provide it to you. Get your affirmation from yourself. Encourage yourself. Tell yourself how well you're doing.

Do not expect raises and benefits other than those agreed upon when you took the job. If you want a raise, make yourself more valuable to your employer and then ask for a raise. DO NOT ASK for a raise because you need more money, you have bills to pay, you can't make it on the pay you're receiving or any other reason that begins with "you." Frankly, none of your personal issues are relevant to the company you work for. What is relevant is the value added to the company by what you do for it. So, ask for more money when you have learned additional skills, mastered the work given to you (meaning you're doing it error-free), accomplished more than you were hired to do, exceeded your supervisors' or customers' expectations, and ultimately made yourself more valuable to your employer.

Do not expect personal friendships at work. It's nice if you do make friends on the job, but don't expect your job to supply your personal friendships, romantic attachments, and social life, or to fulfill your emotional needs. If you have those expectations of co-workers, you'll likely find yourself disappointed. When personal relationships on the job go sideways, your job could be in jeopardy. For example, many co-workers flirt with one another and get romantically involved. Close personal relationships between co-workers often adversely affect work performances, which results in lost opportunities for raises and promotions, and sometimes in lost jobs. The smaller the company, the more dangerous it is to have personal relationships on the job.

The root of the issue of relationships with co-workers is that we are trying to feel better about ourselves by being included and wanted by other people. It is a basic human need to feel that we are a part of something bigger than ourselves. Because many of us spend more time with the people at work than we do with our own families, it's easy to fall into the trap of believing that the relationships we have at work are real and long-lasting. In the overwhelming majority of instances, they are not. They are only situational; the relationship will remain as it is as long as the situation remains as it is. For example, when co-workers are dating and one gets a promotion or transferred to another department or another location, the dynamics of the relationship often change, resulting in a shift or an end in the relationship as they have known it.

Two ways to maintain a healthy balance in your relationships with co-workers are to make a decision to get your self-esteem from who you are and your personal achievements, and to make your family and your friendships outside of work high priorities in your life.

BECOME A VALUABLE EMPLOYEE

How do you become the best employee in the company? Develop a good work ethic, which involves being reliable, stable, resourceful, good natured, punctual, knowledgeable, and so much more. It's summed up in the desire to be of service.

One of the many ways to develop good work ethic is to make yourself the most knowledgeable person in the workplace. *How?* On your own time, set up Google alerts for your company, its products and services, the industry, and the competition so that any time there is mention of those things in the media, you'll receive an alert and can read the article. You may learn something valuable that even the CEO of the company isn't yet aware of! You can also invest your personal time in reading the websites of your company, the industry association, the competition, key customers, and vendors. If you read company annual reports and press releases, you'll hear from top management the important issues of the company and industry. Knowledge is power. Rather than spending time watching television, invest some of it in researching your employer, and you'll see a return on that investment that you cannot otherwise earn.

If you're in sales or service, it helps to understand your company's competition. The more you learn and the more valuable you make yourself, the more income you'll generate, whether it's from your present employer or from your next employer or business partners.

For example, imagine that you go to a car dealership to buy a car. If you speak to a sales person who can't answer your questions about the features of the vehicle, you're not likely to buy from that person. If, on the other hand, you are talking with a sales person who knows what every little button and gadget is for and seems to know everything about the vehicle and why it is better than the competition's vehicle, you'll be much more likely to buy from that person. These two types of sales people can be found everywhere. The ones who cannot answer potential customers' questions haven't been denied training or told never to ask any questions about the products they're selling. They are the ones who haven't taken the time to read and learn about the products they're selling. Product information is typically all around us. It's in brochures, on websites, and in the heads of more experienced people around us. All we have to do is intentionally spend our time gathering this information and learn it so that we'll have it when the next prospective customer asks about it. Making ourselves more valuable to the company by becoming more knowledgeable is necessary regardless of your position in the company.

Pay attention to what's going on around you. Listen more than you talk; do what you are expected to do *and extra if you have time*; don't make personal phone calls or do personal things while on the clock.

Punctuality counts. Get to work early or on time every day and give 110% while you're there. Don't take long breaks and lunches, and don't leave work early.

Be willing to do what other employees are reluctant to do – of course, within legal and ethical boundaries. I'm referring to difficult tasks and hard work. The majority of people are only willing to do what they're asked to do and nothing more. If, on the other hand, you're willing to do more than expected, you will be noticed. You will earn opportunities that aren't offered to others; and if someone has to be laid off, it's less likely to be the best employee, YOU.

Be a student. Seek out and gladly receive advice and suggestions for how to improve. Do not act as though you know everything there is to know. As long as you're breathing, you can still learn something. Even if you do already know what's being suggested, be nice, smile, thank the person, and then go on doing the best you can. Highly successful people remain teachable throughout their whole lives. They know they don't know it all.

Be neutral. Try to get optimum results with a minimum of confusion. People who cause strife or chaos, or are involved in it at all, don't get promoted, don't get pay raises, and don't get other good opportunities. Getting optimum results means you're effective on the job. Being effective means doing what you are being paid to do *or more* without making the situation worse or creating some other problem.

It doesn't matter if you're digging ditches in the hot sun or working in an air-conditioned office; do your job with everything you've got and with a smile on your face. Do your job the best you know how to do it, always looking for ways to do it better, faster, more efficiently. Set your "personal best" records for speed and accuracy, and then work to improve your record.

If your boss is looking for someone to fill a position and you are always on time, you always have a smile on your face, you are willing to do whatever needs to be done, you are not wrapped up in drama on the job, and you aren't complaining about things all the time, then you'll probably be considered for the promotion over employees who don't have all those things going for them. In fact, if you have all those attributes but lack the specific experience or skill necessary for that job, you may be given preference over someone who does have the experience or skill, but who has a bad attitude, an attendance problem, or some other issue.

Don't think it's not possible. I've seen it happen. In fact, I've been the one who was given opportunities over other more experienced, more educated people simply because of a good attitude and the willingness to work hard. I've also been the employer who provided education and opportunities to an employee on the basis of attitude and work ethic. Conversely, if you are someone who has a bad attitude, is argumentative or moody, stays out late partying and drags into work the next day (looking like you've been run over by a truck), complains all the time, is frequently late, or calls in sick, you're not likely to be considered for a promotion, raise, or other opportunities that arise.

Do well by doing good. *How?* Focus on being of service to your supervisor, co-workers, and customers. If you finish your work, ask others if you can help them. By doing this, you'll learn more and make yourself more valuable to your co-workers and your employer. The more valuable you are, the more money you will earn. Be willing to make sacrifices if necessary. This means working extra hours or giving up a day off to help your employer meet a deadline or fill a special order. If you do make sacrifices (also known as paying your dues), do it without feeling sorry for yourself. Remember, when you help your employer accomplish the mission of the company, the company is better able to pay salaries, provide benefits, and promote you.

Be your own "PR agent." Tell your boss what a good employee you are and how good you are at doing your job. Chances are that no one else will do it. You have to "self-promote." Point out how you're never late, never take long breaks, never leave early, never call in sick, have a low error rate, and anything else you can think of that is true that will emphasize what a good employee you are. You are your own public relations agent! If you don't promote yourself, the speed of life may interfere with your boss's recognition of your talents.

THE IMPORTANCE OF ATTITUDE

A bad attitude will hold you back from promotions, higher pay, better jobs, and good relationships because people won't want you around. People with bad attitudes bring everyone around them down. They create messes with customers who require damage control. They require constant affirmation, feedback, or supervision. When that's the case, you're a hassle to your employer, boyfriend, girlfriend, spouse, friends, etc. Be easy to be with, easy to get along with, easy to be friends with. How? BE NICE. Don't make everything about you. Think of how what you say or do will make other people feel, and don't say or do anything that will make someone else feel bad. If you do, say you're sorry and really mean it.

My grandfather had a lousy attitude; he was always complaining

SERVING OTHERS IS THE KEY

about being unlucky, being dealt a bad hand, being kicked in the teeth, etc. He was dialed into a self-pity attitude, and until the day he died, he just got more of the same negativity he constantly talked about. He tried several times to break off a piece of the American dream by opening his own businesses. Every attempt was a failure–not because the ideas were flawed, but because his attitude was bad. He always got what he said he was going to get – failure. He expected something bad to happen, and it always did.

One of the businesses he opened was Acme Locksmith. After being injured at his Welfare-to-Work job, which was the post-World War II government's answer to the unemployed (they were expected to <u>do</u> something for a welfare check), the government trained him to be a locksmith and provided the money for the key cutter, key blanks, and pick set. He borrowed money to put an ad in the phone book, and he was in business. So far, so good. Now, factor in the bad attitude.

One weekday afternoon as my grandfather sat in his recliner watching television and complaining that he had no customers, the phone rang. It was a woman who had locked her keys in her car just a few blocks away. She needed a locksmith to come unlock her car. She frantically explained that she had left her kids at home alone for a quick trip to the grocery store, and she accidentally locked herself out of her car. She had walked in the heat to the nearest pay phone and needed help immediately.

My grandfather looked at the clock and told the woman, *"It's 5:05. We closed at 5:00. I can't help you,"* and promptly hung up. Needless to say, someone with a good attitude who was looking for an opportunity to earn a living by helping people would have seen this call as a perfect opportunity to help a person in need while earning a fair wage. Had my grandfather gone to help that lady, not only would he have earned some money that we desperately needed, but the lady might have told others about the good locksmith she'd found, and those people might have called the next time they needed a locksmith. Telling others about your services, known as "word of mouth," is one of the most effective types of marketing a business. My grandfather had missed the opportunity to build a successful business in the most common and least expensive way.

Through the years there were other failed businesses, including having a compost pile that was supposed to grow worms for sale (that only stunk up the area behind the house), raising and selling finch (that generated more bird poop than it did money), and selling various types of trinkets. Unfortunately, my grandfather never even considered the idea of earning a living by helping others. Through all the jobs and business failures, my grandfather never accepted responsibility for his own choices and outcomes nor understood that the world didn't owe him anything.

What my grandfather's complaining taught me is that we're each responsible for our own attitude. It's not that others don't have concern for us. Some do, but they can't fix our problems and they can't make us happy. They usually can't change our circumstances, except perhaps superficially. More importantly, it's not their responsibility to do so.

Successful people CHOOSE to maintain a good attitude. This isn't a passive thing. It's a deliberate action, and it can be very difficult. Anyone can do this when things are going well. It takes a great deal of strength to keep smiles on our faces and to be nice to people around us when we feel like crying or screaming or running away.

Every good waiter or waitress can tell you that if you want to earn good tips, you have to take care of people's wants and needs and do it with a smile and a good attitude. This is true at work and in our relationships. As the salesman and motivational speaker, Zig Ziglar has said in his book, *See You at the Top,* "You can have anything in this life you want if you'll just help enough other people get what they want." Helping meet the needs of others with a smile and a good attitude, without obligation and regardless of what's going on in your own life, is the secret of every good sales person and the basis on which every good service person operates.

There is, in a sense, a type of magnetism that somehow attracts to us whatever attitude we emit. It's as though each of us is a receiver receiving invisible transmissions, not unlike a radio receiving signals from the radio station. Our "receiver" receives the same type of transmissions we send out in the same way that dialing into the rap station gets you rap music and dialing into the country station gets you country music. The station you dial into determines the transmission you receive. So, having a good attitude will attract to you people who have a good attitude. Having a bad attitude will result in people with a good attitude distancing themselves from you (because they don't want to be around someone with a bad attitude), which leaves you surrounded with others who have a bad attitude.

Your desire to dial into a certain attitude will get you that attitude. Failure to decide to have a good attitude doesn't result in no attitude – it results in a bad or negative attitude.

CHAPTER 11

SO WHAT DO YOU WANT?

I mproving your life requires making a decision to have goals, setting specific goals in each area, determining the price you'll have to pay to achieve each goal, and then paying the price.

As you determine what you want, break down how you want to spend your days in terms of your work and your free time, what relationships you want to have, where you want to live, and what things you want to have.

Once you decide specifically what it is you want and create a picture in your mind of what your life will be like once you have reached your goals, your brain will automatically begin to look for opportunities to move you closer to your goals. If you give your brain a question, it'll begin to formulate an answer. *The key is in asking the right question.* For example, if a salesman says to you, *"You don't want to buy this product, do you?"* your mind tends to agree with the premise that you don't want the product. But if the question is, *"What would it take for you to buy this product?"* then your mind begins to think about ways to buy the product. So, ask yourself, "*What do I want?*" Whatever it is, make sure you can see it clearly in your mind's eye. You are not likely to achieve or have anything you cannot clearly see in your imagination as a reality in your life.

DECIDE EXACTLY WHAT YOU WANT

Now that you've taken responsibility for your own life, figure out what it is you want. Establish goals in every area where you have a need or desire to improve your life. For example, you may want to set goals for your career, marriage, friendships, and material things. It's easy to get overwhelmed in this process, but remember that successful people typically work toward the attainment of goals their whole lives. As one goal is achieved, a different goal is set.

Before you set a goal, try to understand all your available options. There are probably careers that you have never even considered because you haven't been exposed to them. There are books in the library and resources on the Internet that you can use to explore the possibilities. There are also resources that can help you determine whether or not you have the aptitude for a particular career. You wouldn't want to spend the time, energy, and money on an education to be an accountant only to find that you hate sitting at a desk working with numbers all day.

Setting material goals will often encourage you to accomplish your career goals faster. The man who hired me when I was 21 often said that he looked for sales people who had lofty goals because he believed they'd do the work necessary to get them. That was certainly true for me.

As you set materials goals like buying a car, buying a house, and so on, don't be discouraged if your goals seem out of reach. They should be slightly out of reach so that you'll have to stretch to get them, but not so much so that attainment seems impossible. If there is something you really want, but you are having trouble visualizing yourself with it, then do something to create the visual image of having the goal.

For example, if there is a specific car you want, put on your best clothes and go to the car dealership to check out the car you think you'd like to have. Sit in it. Explore how the seat feels. Grip the steering wheel. Get the brochure and look at it every day. Have a picture taken of yourself sitting in the car. Look at that car every morning when you first wake up and again before you fall asleep. That's how I went from driving a "theft recovery" Pontiac that I bought at the wrecking yard to a brand new Corvette. I taped a picture of a brand new Corvette on my bathroom mirror so that I'd see it first thing in the morning and last thing at night. Every time I looked at that picture, I imagined myself driving that car. Then I went to the dealership to test drive *my* Corvette so that I knew how it felt to sit behind the wheel, to feel the power as it accelerated, to hear the sound system, and to experience every little detail of that car.

It wasn't very long before that car was mine! Getting the car wasn't magic. What happened as I looked at that picture night and day is that my brain was working overtime trying to figure out how to get that car. Because I was thinking about what I had to do to get that car, I looked for ways to earn extra money. I was motivated to work harder and longer until the day I went down to the dealership and brought "*my car*" home! Use this same visualizing process with all the things you'd like to have.

One cautionary note about this is to not let the desire for material things overtake you. It's great to have a nice home, a comfortable car, and other nice things so long as those things don't become more important than the people in our lives. Relationships are far more important than all the "things" of the world.

If you're someone who thinks that it's too late for you to get what you want, that you've made too many mistakes, or that too much time has gone by, forget all that and take the first step. One person I know took nineteen years to complete her bachelor's degree! Regardless of how long it takes you to achieve your goal, when you do achieve it, it STILL counts!

DETERMINE WHAT IT WILL TAKE TO GET WHAT YOU WANT

Once you know the price of your goal in terms of time, money, and sacrifice, decide whether or not you are willing to do what it takes to get what you want. If you're not willing to pay the price, then you have to change what you want. You may go through this process a number of times before you find the thing that you really want and decide that you are willing to do what it takes to get it.

For example, when I graduated from high school, I thought I wanted to be a lawyer. Since I wanted to be a prosecuting attorney, I went to the library and read through some articles and books written by people who were living that life. What I learned from people who were district attorneys was that the work was difficult, it required long hours, it was stressful, and you often didn't get the conviction you thought should be the result of all that hard work. Furthermore, the pay was much lower than that of lawyers practicing in other areas of the law. Then when I met with my high school counselor, I heard about the requirement of years of law school after completing my bachelor's degree, and I discovered the high cost of law school if I was unable to get a scholarship. It didn't take long before I decided that the many years of college and the financial investment weren't worth the outcome. I was not willing to pay the price.

At the same time I was considering a law career, I was working in an insurance office, which afforded me an "insider's viewpoint" of a career as an insurance broker. It appeared that the nature of the insurance business provided that these men (*and they were all men at that time*) could work hard in the first years of their career, build their clientele, and in the latter years of their career, relax into a less hectic life of taking care of existing clients. It didn't take long to see that if insurance brokers take good care of their clients, their clients renew their insurance policies year after year. Rather than having to go find new clients all the time, the same clients pay you every year to keep them properly protected.

It appeared that prosecuting attorneys have to work just as hard in their latter years as they did in their earlier years, and at the end of their career, they have no business to sell that will supplement whatever retirement plan may be provided. On the other hand, insurance brokers who have taken good care of their clients can sell the businesses they've built for a profit in addition to receiving any other retirement income. I didn't like the ideas of having worked all my life and having nothing to sell and being at the mercy of others for my retirement income. So after comparing these two careers, I decided to learn all I could about being the best possible insurance broker. That became my number one goal.

Once you have an idea of what you think you would like to do, go onto the Internet and search for articles written by and about people who are doing what you think you might want to do. Find out all you can about what their lives are like. Imagine yourself living that life. Is it appealing to you? Are there disadvantages you hadn't previously considered? Does the potential "downside" to that life change your mind about spending your days doing what they do? If so, move on to the next thing you're interested in doing. If not, take the next step and find out what you'll have to do to have the life they have, such as what education, skills, or talents are required. How much time and money will it take to bridge the gap between where you are now and where you'd need to be in order to achieve your goals? What will it cost in terms of time, money, and sacrifice to get the education or skills you need?

Be realistic. It's important to be honest with yourself and consider whether or not you have the talent to do what you're considering doing. For example, given my gender and age, I have no ability to ever play in the NFL! I am a naturally optimistic person, and I've had some amazing things happen for me that seemed at the time to be completely unrealistic, but no amount of optimism or training will ever make me a professional athlete!

You cannot be a surgeon if you can't stand to see blood. You can't be a professional athlete or a musician if you don't have an element of natural talent and you're not willing to train and practice for hours and hours every day. And, as the show *American Idol* has taught us, only a tiny percentage of the general population has that delicate balance of talent, youth, looks, charisma, and marketability to be a "star." So, at the risk of discouraging you from your dreams, understand that you were put here for a reason. There is a purpose and plan for your life, which includes prosperity and happiness, but it may not include being the best brain surgeon, the next amazing athlete, the new American Idol, the funniest comedian, or an award-winning actor. The plan for your life might not include fame or millions of dollars, BUT you do have exactly what you need to fulfill your individual purpose for living, and it is that specific purpose which will give you a sense of fulfillment.

CREATE YOUR PLAN TO ACHIEVE EACH GOAL

Once you've decided on the goals, you must create a plan for attainment for each one.

If you've ever lived in a house or apartment with a thermostat, you know that you can set the thermostat to a certain temperature. If everything is working correctly, the thermostat causes either heat or cool air to come on automatically to keep the room at the goal temperature. The plan for achieving your goals is like that thermostat. It's a critical part in the successful attainment of your goals.

Once you've gathered enough information, create your plan and a timeline for accomplishment of the plan.

Without a specific plan, most people never reach their goals. Imagine a contractor who sets out to build a house. He doesn't just go buy some lumber and nails and start building a house without considering how big it will be, what style it is, how many bedrooms it will have, etc. Without a definite plan, the contractor who just starts hammering nails into wood is going to wind up with a monstrosity.

To create a beautiful home, the contractor works with an architect to draw up plans that spell out every detail of the house to the point that there is a clear picture of what the finished product will look like – all this before a single nail enters a piece of wood. The contractor purchases the materials necessary to complete the job and then works the plan. If the plan gets changed after the construction has begun, materials are wasted or additional materials have to be purchased, the construction takes much longer, and the whole thing costs much more than it should. The contractor who keeps the vision he or she wants to create in the forefront of his or her mind and measures progress regularly eventually creates and enjoys the subject of his or her vision.

It is keeping your focus on the goal and regularly reviewing the plan and evaluating your progress that will make you stay home and go to bed early rather than going out with your friends on a night when you have to go to work the following morning. It's what will make you go to work when you have a sore throat and don't feel like getting out of bed. It's what will cause you to identify opportunities that others miss.

It's okay to change your goals and your plan for their attainment because you've learned additional information and made a different decision. It isn't failure unless you're just giving up. If you change your goal from one thing to another because you have new information, you're still focused and moving toward a goal.

KEEP FOCUSED ON YOUR GOALS

Once you've decided on what you want, you have a good understanding of the price you're willing to pay to get it, and you have a plan for its achievement, LOCK ON TO THAT TARGET AND HOLD ON LIKE A HUNGRY DOG WITH A BONE! Don't allow anyone or any circumstance to change your mind or distract you from your ultimate goal.

Suppose when you're moving toward your goal, you meet someone and you are distracted or have second thoughts about your goal. Here's the difference between someone who reaches his or her goals and others who don't: People who DO reach their goals get themselves back on track or adjust their goal and begin moving toward the new goal. Either way, they keep moving toward their goals. The ones who never break out of mediocrity are the ones who get distracted and don't ever make a real effort to get back to taking steps toward their goals.

All of us get off track at times. Sometimes it's because we intentionally choose to do something we know we shouldn't do. Most times it's just life's circumstances, such as meeting someone you want to spend time with rather than working toward the goal. It doesn't matter what it is that gets you off track. What matters is that you get yourself back on track. Don't give up. If you do, twenty years from now you'll regret your decision to hang with friends you can barely remember. You'll always wonder what life would've been like. Don't let "shoulda, coulda, woulda" happen to you.

This is so much easier said than done. Even though I had worked hard in high school to earn a four-year college scholarship, I turned that scholarship down because I'd met someone and was willing to throw away my goals for the feeling of love, acceptance, and belonging that I'd never had. My emotional needs far outweighed the goals that seemed so far off and unrealistic at the time. There was no one in my life at the time to suggest to me that if the guy truly loved me, as he said he did, that he'd want me to pursue my dreams and follow my ambitions. In hindsight, I think he didn't want me to pursue a higher education because he was afraid I would outgrow him or meet someone else. It's fairly common for people

Losers focus on what they're going through.
Winners focus on what they're going TO.

to be threatened by others who want more out of life than they do. Unfortunately, people around us will often discourage us from doing something that they are unable or unwilling to do or that will ultimately make them look less successful than us.

I know a man who intentionally chose NOT to go out with his friends or date until he was well on the way toward reaching his financial goals. That kind of resolve takes a lot of strength and determination. Every time friends called to invite him out, he turned them down. It didn't take long before they stopped calling. Although many of his friends are still in the old neighborhood and struggling in their finances and relationships, he ultimately accomplished everything he set out to do and more! Because of the sacrifices he was willing to make while working toward his goals, he now has a great marriage and family, a successful business, and everything else that goes along with the life he intentionally designed.

Be like that man and choose to say no to the temptations of doing anything that will delay your goals. Press through the physical or emotional pain, or whatever illness, issue, or fear you face. Force yourself to act like the person you want to become. Do what's necessary and you can be assured that eventually you WILL reach your goal!

SET TIMELINES FOR MEASURING YOUR GOALS

Set timelines for measurement of your goals. What gets measured gets accomplished. If you fail to set specific times to evaluate your progress, your goals quickly become nothing more than a wish. Write down your specific goals, monitor your progress, make adjustments where necessary, and set new timelines. Keep doing this as long as necessary until you reach the goal.

There might be times in your life that you think you're doing all the right things but it feels like nothing is happening. Remember that just like a seed has to be buried in order to sprout and grow into a tree that bears fruit, there is that time after the seed has been planted in the ground that no one can see the seed or what's happening to it. On the surface it looks like nothing is happening, but in fact roots are sprouting and growing and the soil will break open with a sprout if you wait and keep doing what you're supposed to do. Even when you don't see the results right away, DON'T STOP BELIEVING that you can reach your goals. Don't quit and give up.

The roots of the seeds you've planted are growing and you WILL see measurable results if you stick with it long enough.

SETBACKS

Many people won't continue moving toward their goals when they don't see measurable results. Others experience setbacks or fail at a goal and then give up completely. Remember, losers by definition lose. Mediocre people get mediocre results. Extraordinary people get extraordinary results.

Most people look at a situation and see the obstacles, problems, and reasons why something is too difficult to do. Extraordinary people see challenges and opportunities. Those of us who have been through adversity have the ability to turn difficult challenges into opportunities. Our experiences have already qualified us as extraordinary. It is up to us to take the "tuition of pain" we've paid and turn it into extraordinary results.

I've experienced many setbacks. In the early years of my business, I would work for months without pay, hoping to make the sale, only to have the prospect choose another option. An employee stole a credit card from my purse and charged furnishings for an office she was opening to compete with me. Another time I spent thousands of dollars putting together an insurance company deal that was to be exclusively mine. Eventually, the insurance company gave the program to another broker, and the program I helped create became my competition.

In the years since 1989 when I started my first business, there have been too many setbacks to mention here. There were times when I felt so defeated, I just wanted to go home and go to bed. There were times when I was so angry, I was probably at risk of having a stroke! There were times when if I had started crying, I wouldn't have been able to stop. Through it all, the reason I didn't quit and give up was that I knew that crying wasn't going to change the situation. Going to bed and staying there would only make things worse. Getting angry gave my control away to the people who had done me wrong. The bottom line was that allowing anger or depression to take over was not an option. Giving in to my emotions was a luxury I could not afford. I had no safety net. I had no one to help me, so I had to refuse to be defeated, remind myself of my goals, and speak only positive words. Ultimately I realized that the coping mechanisms I'd learned in that abusive environment were the very things that made me successful in the face of nearly overwhelming obstacles.

If you try something and fail, consider that it's better to suffer the humiliation of a failed attempt for a while than to regret giving up for a lifetime. I encourage you to fear regret more than you fear failure. Chances are that even if you fall short of the original goal, you'll be better off than you were when you started.

As you're learning to think and act differently and to set goals and begin to move toward them, mistakes are inevitable. It took your whole life for things to be the way they are now, so don't expect to change it all in one day. Recognize that it's a process and give yourself credit for every positive change.

Michael Jordan failed to make a shot thousands of times. But we don't think of him as a failure. We think of him as one of the greatest basketball players ever. He was great because he took the shots. He didn't let the times when he missed cause him to pull back in fear of not making another shot. He went right on and took the next shot. If you "miss a shot," so to speak, at work, in a personal relationship, in trying to start a business, or in any situation, don't quit your job, decide never to have another close friend, decide never to date, or determine never to start another business. Instead, learn from what happened, take an honest look at your role in the debacle, and consider what you could have done differently for a better result. Then get right back in the game and try again.

When you suffer setbacks, it can be particularly difficult to see people who have what you are working so hard to get. When that happens, it's easy to get discouraged, angry, jealous and frustrated. If they earned what they have the right way, swallow your pride and ask their advice. But if they made their money in wrong ways, remember that they may have "things," but they don't have good relationships, good health, peace, and true joy to go with it despite appearances. There is a big difference between pleasure and true happiness. One lasts for a short time and the other endures a lifetime. The conditional pleasure that comes from enjoying the things we have can be over the instant that your car is wrecked, your house burns down, or things you value are stolen. But relationships, health, peace and joy endure through all the trials of life. Choose to succeed the right way.

PROPER PERSPECTIVE FOR YOUR GOALS

In the pursuit of your goals, be careful not to get emotionally tied to what you want, especially material things. Relationships with people you care about are more important than any of the things on your list. So, be careful not to sacrifice time with people you love in order to have a bigger house, a nicer car, special wheels on the car, or any of the other things that many people think they *have to have*. The truth is that you don't *have to have* those things. But one thing you do need to have for fulfillment, peace of mind, and true happiness is a good relationship with the people in your life.

I didn't say you couldn't have a nice car, a beautiful house, or any of the other things you want. But when you value relationships more, the relationships will be better. The ironic thing is that if you're doing all the things I've recommended, you'll wind up with all the things you want without having sacrificed your family, your health, or your peace of mind to get them! You'll enjoy all your *things* more when you have good relationships with people you love.

OVERCOME OBSTACLES

If goals are worth reaching, YOU MUST GO THROUGH difficult circumstances. You don't get to go over, under, or around difficulties. There is no way other than THROUGH difficulties. They are inevitable. That's not to say that you can't see some of them coming; you can – and you can avoid the avoidable difficulties and mitigate the damage of others.

The bigger the goal, the more difficult the circumstances you'll face. If it were easy, everyone would do it.

While I was still "paying my dues" by working for someone else, I had a co-worker who didn't like me and who tried to deter me from achieving my goals. She wanted the opportunity I'd been given and resented that it hadn't been offered to her. What she didn't know or understand was that I wasn't just chosen out of the general population to receive the opportunity for the job I was doing. I had the job I was doing because I had been bold, took a chance, and did what most people wouldn't do in calling and making the offer to work for free. Because I had made such a bold offer to the agency owner, he invested time in mentoring me. Until he retired, he'd single me out of the over forty employees in the agency and occasionally take me to lunch. When he did, I listened intently to everything he said, considering those words as nuggets of wisdom. I took the advice and applied it, and the results were measurable.

That job and the mentoring I received provided a great opportunity for me, but it created a tremendous amount of resentment among my female co-workers and a challenge to me. They were all in positions comparable to secretaries and I was the only female sales associate. As a sales associate, I was meeting with prospects and clients, going out on appointments to gather information and present quotes. I had the opportunity to make commissions in addition to my salary. I was able to compete in sales contests that rewarded winners with gifts and trips. On the surface it didn't look fair. But the truth was that no other woman had ever been given the job because no other woman had ever been bold enough to ask for it.

The ladies in the office didn't include me in conversations in the break room or offers to go out for lunch. I was never invited to bridal or baby showers, housewarming parties, or any other outings that all the other ladies were invited to attend. The other sales associates in the office, all men, didn't include me in their group either. They'd go out to lunch, go shoot pool at lunch time, or have a beer after work. I wasn't included in anything the guys did. So, I worked through my lunch, ran errands, or sat by myself and read or listened to books on tape.

The co-worker who was so jealous of me talked about me behind my back to the others. She told terrible things about me, most of which were untrue. When flowers were delivered to me from a client thanking me for going to bat for his company in getting a premium discount, this co-worker would tell everyone that I must have slept with the client! She walked past my desk and intentionally knocked a cup of coffee all over the files and paperwork I had spread out on my desk. She took a beautiful pen off of my desk that had been given to me by one of the insurance companies I worked with as a reward for a specific task I'd accomplished for them. When a door that was supposed to remain locked was left open one night, this same gal wasted no time going to my supervisor to say that she was certain that I'd left the door unlocked, when in truth I hadn't even been in the office the day the door was left unlocked!

I tell you all this to let you know that I am well aware of the fact that there are people in the world who will do just about anything to prevent you from getting the success that is coming to you. The truth is that there will always be people who don't want to see you succeed. You can't do anything to prevent people like that from being in your workplace and putting obstacles in your path. But you do have control over what you choose to think, say, and do about it. If you let them get to you, you'll be deterred or prevented altogether from reaching your goals – and then they've won. BUT if you choose to look at them as the jealous people they are and go right on about the work required to reach your goals, you'll get what you want.

In the case of the co-worker I told you about, she ultimately quit and moved on, and my other co-workers eventually realized that I wasn't so bad after all! Remember, if people don't have the truth about you, give it to them. If they choose not to believe it, it's their problem. You know the truth about you. Stand on it, regardless of what anyone else does, says, or even thinks about you!

When obstacles arise, setbacks occur, or jealous people try to sabotage you, or when you feel like giving up on your goals, remember:

- Commit yourself to treating people right and making right choices regardless of what others are doing or what the circumstances are.

- Do a good job and be proud of your work, whatever it is.

- Accept your obligations.

- Learn from the situation. Make any necessary adjustments to your goal, its timeline, or the plan for its achievement; then try again. The obstacle or setback is the tuition you paid for the education you are getting. Don't miss the opportunity to mine the lessons out of it and benefit from the wisdom that comes from it.

- Don't give in to self-pity.

- Don't burn up your energy in anxiety.

- Try to please others, but "be okay" with the fact that no matter what you do, some people are never going to love you and approve of you. Some people don't even love themselves, so they're not capable of truly loving someone else.

- Even in the most discouraging times, keep on getting up, believe in yourself, and work to convince others to believe in you.

What's holding you back from achieving your goals? Here are some typical excuses:

- You weren't born into money. You came from a poor family.

- You didn't get the education you wanted.

- You are physically handicapped.

- You were labeled with some mental health diagnosis.

- You have bad credit or no credit at all.

- You had children early in life.

- You see no meaning to your life.

There is one thing that all truly successful people know, and although it's elusive to most people, it isn't a secret. This IS the key that will start the ignition to the vehicle that will take you where you want to go in life. The key to getting where you want to go and to having what you want to have is... *get ready... this is BIG...*

NEVER GIVE UP!

That means that once you've begun to work the plan to achieve your goals, you don't change your mind because you don't feel like going to work. You don't quit a job without another one lined up regardless of the reason. You don't give up on a relationship because the other person made a mistake. You don't quit working toward your goals because of a setback. Get the idea? Go for what you want without giving up, without letting anything distract you, or without letting anyone change your mind, discourage you, or get in your way.

Constantly remind yourself of your goals, such as the car you will have one day, the house you will own, the family you will

What you think about and talk about comes about!
When you desire success and assert your claim to it,
you can then go get it.

have, or whatever it is you're working toward. Remind yourself constantly why you're doing what you're doing, and it'll give you the internal motivation to keep going. Get a folder or a notebook and keep in it pictures from magazines or brochures of houses, cars, boats, families (or what you imagine the family you want would look like), notes of appreciation from clients, or whatever it is you want, and look at them every day. The "*why*" of what you do is the fuel that will keep you going when there's nothing in you that feels like going on.

When you go through the inevitable difficulties on your way to the achievement of each goal, remember that one phone call or one "chance" meeting with someone can change everything. You can literally bump into someone who offers you a wonderful job or business opportunity or who ultimately becomes your spouse or the best friend you've ever had!

FEAR

Many people fear failure so much so that they decide not to set any goals for themselves. They figure that if they don't ever try, they won't feel bad when they don't obtain the object of their desire. It's true that you may not achieve every single goal you set for yourself. But any goal-oriented person will tell you that you will obtain much more with a specific, written goal than you will without it. And half of something is better than all of nothing!

Think about it. If you are renting a 900-square-foot apartment and your goal is to own a 3000-square-foot house but you wind up owning a 2500-square-foot house, you didn't "fail" because you are 500-square-feet short! You still have more than before!

Some people struggle with the idea of being successful. If by now you haven't begun to write out some things you would like to achieve in different areas of your life, ask yourself these questions:

1. Am I afraid of what people will say or think if I fail? *Or if I succeed?*

2. Do I think I don't deserve to have what I want?

3. Do I have a negative image of people who are "successful"?

4. Am I afraid success will change me?

5. Am I afraid of losing success once I have it?

6. Do I believe success will create more problems for me than it's worth?

7. Do I think my relationships will change if I am "successful" and the people in my life are where they have always been?

Ultimately, we'll either work toward our goals or work toward the accomplishment of the goals of others. Choose to be a winner by choosing to set goals, focus on them, and work toward their attainment. Quit dwelling on your past and any excuses that go along with it. Begin today.

CHAPTER 12

MAKE MONEY WORK FOR YOU

Y ou must prepare to be wealthy. It doesn't just happen. It's a deliberate choice, and even people who receive sudden windfalls through inheritance or winning the lottery will typically lose what they instantly acquired because they aren't prepared to handle wealth.

Dare to imagine how you'll feel when you have the things you want. Gather the information, get the facts, and know your options now so that when money starts showing up, you don't get overwhelmed or confused and make bad decisions. Notice that I said "wealthy," not "rich." Riches are temporary but wealth denotes a sense of financial stability. True wealth is much more than temporary cash.

BELIEFS ABOUT MONEY

Our attitude about money acts as an important variable in whether or not we have it, have enough of it, handle it responsibly when we get it, and keep it long-term. So, to get to the point that you have enough of it to accomplish all your goals, you must overcome any attitudes that may keep you from getting and keeping it.

Some people have an aversion to wealth because of negative comments they've heard about wealthy people or the experience of seeing a wealthy person act like a jerk. I was one of those. When I was a young girl, I was taught that money is the root of all evil and that I should be skeptical of people who had it. I was told that people with money probably did something illegal to get it, so they weren't to be trusted. I wasn't interested in having more money than I needed to be comfortable until I met the man who hired me when I was 21. As I got to know Fred, a wealthy man who was honest and hardworking, I realized that what I'd been taught simply wasn't true.

I learned that I could be wealthy and should aspire to be wealthy not only to have the lifestyle I wanted, but to be able to create employment to give others an opportunity to reach their goals and do things for others that I would not otherwise have the means to do. Prior to meeting Fred, I'd never imagined that being wealthy was a possibility for me. After learning that Fred hadn't always been in the top 1% of wage earners, but had started in the insurance business after returning from the military, selling life insurance policies door-to-door, I thought, *"Why not me?"*

Even after I began to acquire the financial rewards of my hard work, it was years before I felt okay about having money. I felt bad for those who had less than I did, so I gave a lot of money to employees, clients, and child advocacy groups. It felt great to do it, but in hindsight, I know now that a big part of why I made some of the decisions I made was that I was uncomfortable with having money and all the things that I was able to buy with it.

I've since learned that the Bible does not say that *"money is the root of all evil."* It actually says, *"The love of money* is the root of all evil" (1 Timothy 6:10). I've also learned that when Jesus said, "It is easier for a camel to go through the eye of a needle than for a rich man to enter the kingdom of God" (Mark 10:25), He was talking about people who trust more in their money than in Him, and who, if made to choose, would choose their money over God. I now know that there is nothing wrong with having money, so long as money doesn't have me.

We've all heard of lottery winners, performers, and athletes who were rich for a limited time only to find themselves penniless. Perhaps it's because they didn't have a good financial plan or a good team of advisors, or because of the family members and friends who expected the person to share. I suspect that people who are at their core uncomfortable with money, like I was, will nearly always sabotage themselves by spending recklessly, giving to a fault, gambling, or simply "frittering it away" until they're back in their comfort zone.

After you've done all you know to do to position yourself to reap the kind of rewards you want, prepare yourself for prosperity by changing the way you think, speak, and act about money. For example, if you have always thought, *"Rich people are all crooks,"* then begin to change that thought to, *"Although there are some dishonest people with money, most people with true wealth are honest, hardworking people who deserve every dollar they've earned because they were willing to put in the extra hours, make the commitment, and take the calculated risks necessary to produce their financial reward."* This way, when you are one of those "rich" people, you won't feel wrong for having more than you need to survive.

If you do want to be wealthy, do what people who went from poverty to wealth did to earn their money. What I'm going to tell you sounds simple, and it is, BUT it isn't always easy.

INVEST, DON'T SPEND

Wealthy people purchase ASSETS rather than liabilities. People who struggle financially their whole lives typically aren't "dealt a bad hand" or aren't "unlucky." They never get rich because they spend what money they have on activities and things that are worthless or soon become worthless rather than purchasing things that generate an income and/or increase in value. For example, if I had spent money on clothes, eating out, or other things that wouldn't help me earn a living or that would decrease rather than increase in value, I would never have been able to purchase the assets that generated the income that allowed me to purchase the houses, cars, clothes, and vacations I enjoy now.

The sacrifice I made in delaying the purchase of some of the things I wanted in order to buy my first office building was one of the best decisions that I ever made. That building generated a monthly income of rents from the tenants and saved thousands of dollars in rent that I had been paying to the owner of the office space I previously rented. When I sold it, I received in profit about the same amount as I paid for the building. While I was saving rent money by operating my businesses out of that building and receiving rental income from tenants, the building doubled in value!

Had I continued to pay office rent, I'd have just been giving thousands of dollars away to the person who owned the building. I wanted to be the one who owned the building and collected the rent! In making the sacrifice not to buy whatever I wanted as soon as I had the money for it, I was able to purchase property that ultimately generated much more income than any of those things I did without would ever have been worth.

I know what it feels like to want something and have no ability to get it. I know what it feels like to have a few dollars and to be tempted to buy things I'd like to have that are now within reach, but that fall far short of what I really want. Remember, you cannot reach your desired goals if you spend money on distractions.

From the time I bought my first house when I was 18, being a property owner was more important to me than having the hottest jeans or newest shoes, going out to dinner, or driving a nicer car – especially when the car I could've afforded at the time was still a long stretch from the car I *really* wanted. I don't like the feeling of settling for less than what I really want when I can come up with a plan and then work the plan to get exactly what I want. Doing without in the meantime is a necessary part of eventually getting what you really want. Too few people really understand that; or if they do understand, too few are willing to do without while working toward the goal.

Many people spend their money on the things they want, justifying it by saying, *"It's only a few dollars." "I've earned it." "What's the big deal anyway?"* The big deal is that each dollar spent on something that could have been purchased less expensively, or was unnecessary, is a dollar that you can't use to buy or invest in the things that can earn a return on your investment.

You may think you don't make enough money to save any of it. Suppose you save $100 by keeping a dollar or two out of every paycheck, by working overtime, by looking for opportunities to make a little extra money, and by offering to do something for someone for a fair payment. You can choose to take that $100 and go out to a nice dinner OR you can take that $100 and make an investment in something that you can sell for more than $100, begin an investment account at a discount brokerage, or start an interest-earning bank account. When you choose to save and invest, you begin to think like wealthy people do.

Wealthy people are always looking for good investments. When an opportunity presents itself, they measure the possible return on investment with the potential risk of losing their money, and if the possible return is greater than the risk, they go for it. Then with the income generated by their investments, they purchase the luxury items they want.

Here's an example of finding a good opportunity for investment. While working in the insurance office, I had a client whose vehicle was stolen. After thirty days of waiting for the vehicle to be recovered, the insurance company paid my client for the value of the stolen and unrecovered vehicle. Just a few days after the client was paid and had purchased another car, the stolen vehicle was found. I hadn't seen this happen before and was curious as to how the insurance company would handle the situation.

The insurance company claims adjuster told me that their payment to the client entitled them to the ownership of the recovered vehicle. She went on to say that since they are not in the business of used car sales, they sell the cars for salvage to wrecking yards. This gave me an idea to go to a wrecking yard and look at salvaged vehicles to see if any were structurally sound and could be fixed up, cleaned up, and sold for a profit.

I went to the junkyard and saw that there were plenty of "theft recovery" cars that needed things like seats, dashboards, sound systems, and paint jobs, but they ran just fine. I was in my early twenties and my money was tied up in two houses, so I had no cash with which to buy or repair the cars. So I asked the owner of the junkyard if he would be interested in a partnership. I did the same thing with a mechanic and a paint and body man. My role was to advertise and sell the finished product. Ultimately, we were a group of four with each person contributing something. Only one was contributing cash, and that was the owner of the wrecking yard. Everyone made a good return on his or her investment, which was a revenue stream for each of us in addition to the salary from our employment.

With profits from sold vehicles, we began to purchase houses, fix them up, and sell them for a profit. All of us received a share of the profit in direct proportion to the investment we had made in the property. If the person was only in for 1% of the value of the house, he or she received 1% of the profit. This allowed people who didn't have very much money to get involved in purchasing a property that they could not otherwise afford, and we generated profit that could be rolled into the next project, which in turn would generate more profit.

Let's clarify one thing about investing. Many people buy cars, jewelry, antiques, and collectibles and call them investments. But unless you're purchasing the item at an amount far below true market cost and planning to sell the item, just be honest and call it what it is – spending. A real investment will generate income or will be more valuable in the future than when you purchased it.

WAIT!

Wealthy people wait patiently for what they want. Quit saying, *"I've worked hard and I deserve this." "I'll just buy this and figure out how to pay for it later." "I don't know how I'm going to pay for this, but somehow it'll all work out."* People with this kind of attitude show that they aren't mature enough to wait until they can truly afford something before they buy it. People who have acquired wealth do not expect that someone is going to come along and magically fix everything for them. What you need to do is take responsibility for your own decisions. Make the right decision to do without something for the time being, and you won't need anyone to come along and fix everything for you later.

Learn to wait until you can afford the thing you want. This means not buying expensive clothes and jewelry, or *designer* coffee, or any meal that totals more than a few dollars until you have accomplished the big goals you're working toward. Get your priorities straight. You don't need to get every new cell phone. You don't need 800 minutes a month with three-way calling and every other available option unless your income depends on your use of your cell phone. People lived well without cell phones for years. Many very successful people refuse to carry a cell phone! If you choose to have one, make it work for you. In other words, use your cell phone to get and keep your job, increase your income, and maintain your relationships.

For years I had a postcard pinned in my cubicle of a beautiful Mercedes SL with the top down, just beginning to pull out from a parking space in front of a high-end store on Rodeo Drive in Beverly Hills. I'd never been to Beverly Hills and I certainly couldn't afford anything from any store on Rodeo Drive. But every day I looked at that picture and said, *"That's going to be me someday."*

> *Put off getting what you want,*
> *at least for now.*

My co-workers thought I was crazy (and told me so) because while I was predicting my future prosperity, I was driving a beat-up car with bald tires and no air conditioning in Southern California, where summer temperatures are frequently over 100°. I looked at that postcard for years as I drove cars that had come from the wrecking yard. As time went on, I could have afforded the car payment on a newer car; I could have stretched myself financially and bought an *economy car* that wouldn't have been the embarrassment that some of those "wrecking yard" cars were. Although I was able to make a car payment, I chose to save and invest my money and continue to drive those old, beat-up cars for a little while longer. Waiting for what I really wanted is the reason I drive the cars I have now. Had I bought a nicer car back then, I wouldn't have been able to save money for the down payment on my first rental property. If I hadn't bought the first house, I wouldn't have made the profit that enabled me to buy the next house and the next house, and then the first office building, which finally led me to where I am now. Eventually, after achieving many of my goals, I did get that beautiful, new Mercedes SL convertible.

BUYING WISELY

Wealthy people do not buy on emotion. Immature people and those who do not manage their money effectively tend to make emotional decisions and impulse purchases as a way to make themselves feel better. Unfortunately, it's only a temporary fix. After the item is purchased and the excitement is gone, so is the money. A very typical example of this would be seeing a car you just have to have, walking into the dealership, finding out that you qualify for a loan, and driving off in that car. I've made that mistake myself. But I guarantee that even though I now can walk onto any car dealership and purchase almost any vehicle, I will never make a "big ticket" impulse purchase again.

When I decide I want a new car, I do the research to compare all the options of all the vehicles that I'm interested in, and I decide what features are truly important to me and what features may sound good but are irrelevant to me. Then I compare prices of available vehicles at dealerships across the country, narrow my choice down to two or three options, and negotiate with the sales manager (*never with sales people*) of the dealerships. I typically save thousands of dollars by doing this rather than by walking onto the lot of the nearest dealer. I can save even more by searching the Internet for a slightly used car that has all the features I want without the huge depreciation that follows the purchase of a brand new car.

Wealthy people do not buy anything without careful consideration of all the factors involved. Specifically:

1. Research the price on the Internet and find the best listed price of the item you're trying to buy.

2. Search the Internet for coupons, promotions, and discount codes for the item. This can save you a lot of money.

3. On "big ticket" items like cars, call the place with the best listed price for the item and negotiate your best deal over the phone. This will help you avoid impulsive, emotional purchases. If you're not sitting in the car smelling the "new car smell" and touching the steering wheel, you'll be less likely to take the first deal offered.

4. If an item is something you need that will help you make money, such as appropriate clothes for your job, a tool, a PDA to help you get organized, etc., consider shopping at a discount store, a consignment store, or online (which is like an enormous "yard sale") to get what you need at the lowest possible price.

It's been reported that Sam Walton of WalMart and Sam's Club, who was one of the wealthiest men in the United States, drove an older model pickup and lived in the same modest house nearly all his adult life. Surely it was a nice house, but not the spectacular mansion that he could clearly afford. Why would a man who could drive a different Ferrari every day of the year drive an average car or live in an average house? *Because he was confident in himself and he had nothing to prove.*

WHEN TO USE CREDIT

Wealthy people use *other people's money* (credit) only when the cost of the item PLUS the interest on the money borrowed is less than the value or anticipated value of the item purchased, or when the item is necessary to earn your living.

Unless you and your family will starve to death between the time you are broke and payday, don't borrow money from anyone, especially from those payday advance places, unless it's to purchase something that will generate income. You can do without just about everything. Out of gas? Ride the bus, catch a ride with someone, borrow a bike, or walk.

When you borrow money or buy an item with a credit card, you incur interest – *unless you pay the entire balance when the bill comes*. When you calculate the interest and add it to the sales price, anything you purchase with the borrowed money costs <u>more</u> than the price on the tag. I'm sure you'll agree that it's not very smart to walk into a store and pay MORE than the asking price. So, before you purchase anything with borrowed money, whether it be on a credit card, payday advance loan, a bank loan, or money borrowed from someone, do what wealthy people do and calculate the "true cost" of the item you're considering purchasing.

If you do borrow money, regardless of whether it's by using a credit card or in any other way, ALWAYS repay your debt. Even if you have to make arrangements to pay your debt for the next twenty years, pay something toward what you owe each month. The sooner you are able to pay your entire balance every month, the sooner you'll have true financial success. If you borrow money to make purchases based on emotional or impulsive desires, you'll probably never have financial success.

When determining whether to make an outlay of cash or to take on debt, ask yourself:

- Will the money that I spend get me something that will increase in value?

- Will this purchased item help me to make money, such as a bicycle or a car, to get to and from work?

- Will this purchased item cause me to lose more money than the money spent on it? If so, is buying the item worth the loss?

If the answer to any of these questions is "yes," then follow these guidelines, especially if you are buying a car or another "big ticket" item:

1. Ask for the best price if you were to buy the item with cash. Even though you probably don't have the cash, you'll likely get their "real" lowest price if you ask what their best price is for someone who walks in today and makes a cash offer.

2. Never shop some place just because they advertise easy credit or credit for someone with a poor credit history. If you go to a bank and get yourself approved for a specified amount of credit ahead of time, you'll likely be able to negotiate a better deal. You can find first-time buyer loans for real estate, vehicle financing with no credit or poor credit, business loans, etc., by shopping on the Internet.

3. Once you've found the names of some finance companies or banks that are located near you, invest the time in calling those places. Yes, it will likely take more time than just walking onto a car lot and taking whatever financing the dealer offers to buyers, but you'll pay hundreds to thousands of dollars less in fees and interest charges if you

obtain financing yourself. Imagine paying someone a couple thousand dollars to do this search on the Internet and make the calls for you. That's exactly what you'll be doing if you go to a car lot and pay the dealership to secure your financing for you.

4. Regardless of where your financing comes from, never take the first deal offered. Walk away – even if it's for thirty minutes to take a walk down the street. Clear your head WITHOUT looking at the item and really think about what it would be like to have it. Will you use it? How often? Is there a better deal to be made somewhere else?

5. When you think you've negotiated your best deal, walk away. That's right. Walk away. Then you'll find out if it really was the best deal. It is easy to get caught up in the excitement of buying a new item, but often you are still paying for it long after it is no longer useful to you. Salespeople will often call you back or run after you to give you an even lower price when they know they have someone who is ready to make a deal, is qualified to make a deal (because you've already gotten your own financing lined up), and is willing to walk away to make a better deal somewhere else. If they don't chase after you to lower the price, and if you already know from your Internet search that their price is a good one, then, AND ONLY THEN, agree to the deal.

6. If you're considering going into debt for something, figure out how much you will have paid by the end of the loan. Multiply the monthly payment by the length of time it'll take you to pay it off and determine if what you're thinking of buying is still a good deal. For example, a car purchased for $2,500 that is financed could add up to a total outlay of over $5,000. With the purchase of a vehicle, consider

SUCCEED BECAUSE OF WHAT YOU'VE BEEN THROUGH

the costs of gas, insurance, tires, and servicing. There are dramatic differences in the costs of service for different makes of vehicles. Also, insurance on one type of vehicle can be much more than on another type of vehicle. Call around for insurance quotes BEFORE purchasing a car.

ASK FOR SPECIAL EXCEPTIONS

Wealthy people confidently ask for what they want. There may be times when you are turned down for something that is a critical part of the achievement of your goals. When these things happen, don't just take "no" for the final answer. Sometimes, you will have to "sell yourself" before getting the answer you want.

For example, if a bank won't open a checking or savings account for you, or if they've turned you down for financing, ask nicely to see the bank manager. Shake that person's hand, look her (or him) in the eyes with a smile, introduce yourself (always using your first and last name), and calmly explain to that person the situation and why she should make an exception for you. Tell the manager that you're a good person; tell her about your job (this emphasizes that you're employed and that you have the means to keep your account going or repay a loan); offer to give names and numbers of people who will vouch for your character; and tell her that you're not looking for sympathy but you want a break. Finally, tell the person that if she does take a chance on you, she won't be sorry and that you won't let her down.

If you are denied your request, do not get angry. Remember, employees are being paid to act in the best interest of their employer. The guidelines of some places simply won't allow for exceptions, but employees often know of their competitors that have different guidelines. Ask if they were in your position, where would they try to get financing or open an account. Regardless of the answer, thank them for their time, and act on any good suggestions or advice that was given. Keep trying until you get what you want. Eventually, you will meet someone who has been where you are or who respects your efforts and will give you a chance.

This same principle applies in many different scenarios. I recently heard a story about a lady who needed a place for her and her children to live, but she didn't have enough of a deposit for a decent apartment in the kind of neighborhood she wanted to live in. She went from one apartment complex to the next, but was turned down by forty different apartment managers. Amazingly, she didn't give up! Most people would give up on looking for an exception after three or four tries. Although she became discouraged, she didn't give up completely. Finally, she found an apartment manager willing to make an exception for her and allow her to rent without a deposit. Her persistence paid off!

When people make an exception for you, thank them genuinely and promise never to let them down. Then, live up to that promise.

LEARN HOW TO MULTIPLY YOUR MONEY

Wealthy people have learned how to multiply their money. What do I mean? After you've paid your bills each month, put away something for your more expensive goals or for an investment. Even if it's 25 cents, put some money away out of every paycheck. When you have $5 saved, look for something that you can buy low and sell for more. You don't have to have $100,000 before you become an "investor." You can take $5 and go to a yard sale to buy something that can be cleaned up or fixed up and sold for $10. If you take $5 every week and are able to find a way to double it weekly without spending the proceeds, in six months you would have $167,772,160! *Check the math. The law of multiplication is amazing.*

Of course, actually doubling your money weekly is virtually

impossible, but a more practical example would be that if you have $1, and you double it within a month, and then you take the $2 and double it the following month, and so on, at the end of the first year, you'd have $2,048. If you start with $10 and double your money monthly, you'll have $20,480 by the end of the first year!

MONTH	START W / $1	START W / $5	START W / $10
1	$1	$5	$10
2	$2	$10	$20
3	$4	$20	$40
4	$8	$40	$80
5	$16	$80	$160
6	$32	$160	$320
7	$64	$320	$640
8	$128	$640	$1,280
9	$256	$1,280	$2,560
10	$512	$22,560	$5,120
11	$1,024	$5,120	$10,240
12	$2,048	$10,240	$20,480

Once you have a little money put away, you have several options to multiply your money:

Start your own business. This doesn't have to be complicated. You simply look for a need that isn't being met or a problem that needs to be solved, and you try to come up with a way to meet the need or solve the problem. It doesn't necessarily take a lot of money, experience, higher education, or other people. It could be as simple as cleaning someone's house or office, washing windows, mowing lawns, detailing cars, running errands, or babysitting. You don't have to go far to find someone who needs help. Not everyone has the means or desire to pay for help, but there are those who will gladly pay for a trustworthy person to help them.

For example, is there an older or disabled person who needs his or her lawn mowed? A busy executive who needs his car washed? A single parent who needs someone to babysit her children? I know someone who babysat for the children of a flight attendant who left her home at 3:00 a.m. This person slept a few hours, got the kids up, fed them, got them off to school, and then went on about his day. It didn't take much time and wasn't difficult work. The flight attendant was grateful for the help and paid generously for it.

You'll find many opportunities to earn money when you think about the needs of others rather than focusing solely on your own. In case the type of work I mentioned isn't appealing to you, consider the fact that the businesses of cleaning homes and offices, window cleaning, and grounds maintenance are multi-million dollar industries.

You can sell items that you find at close-out sales, yard sales, and discount stores online in venues like eBay and Craig's List. These online sales sites broaden your number of potential buyers to literally millions of people around the world. Prior to the Internet, the numbers of potential buyers for whatever you were selling was limited to the number of people you could talk to or see. And you had to have specific knowledge about a product to know if you were picking it up at a price that would allow for profitable resale. With the Internet, you can check to see what something is actually selling for in "real time" before buying it in the hopes for a profitable resale. The Internet makes a "business without walls," meaning little or no overhead costs, almost instantly possible. The amazing resource of the Internet for buying low and selling for a profit cannot be overstated.

I know a very successful business woman who paid for her college tuition to USC by selling a privately labeled line of cosmetics online. On the surface of it, this may not sound remarkable; but at the time she set up her business on eBay and contracted with a cosmetics company to have a line of products labeled with her company's name, she was 16 years old! She was living on her own, going to USC, and working part-time! On top of that, English was not her first language. That very resourceful woman graduated from USC and is now a successful realtor in Orange County, California.

Invest in stocks or bonds. You can set up an investment account with a discount brokerage firm with a fairly small amount of money. There are some investments that are stable and safe, and they yield somewhat more than a bank savings account would yield. The more risk you're willing to take, the more return you may receive. Sound like gambling? In a way, it is.

There are no guarantees that the company you invest in won't file bankruptcy in the future. If that happens, your investment could be worth nothing. One way to minimize the risk is to purchase shares of a mutual fund. A mutual fund contains the stock of many different companies.

Set up your investment account with a company like Schwab that provides free research on companies and analysis of the factors that influence the profitability of the stocks you're considering. It takes only minutes to read their stock analysts' recommendations. They make it easy because they evaluate the stocks and make recommendations about whether or not they consider the stock a good buy. They are experts who are able to spend much more time than you evaluating opportunities. Don't waste your time trying to be an expert in an area when you can get expert advice and guidance at little or no cost.

Imagine investing in a stock that was offered at $3 that increased to $40, $50 or more. In this example, an initial investment of $100 grows in value to $1,333, $1,666 or more!

Don't confuse calculated risk-taking with gambling. Investing in the stock market, in a business deal, in real estate, etc., is only to be done when the probable, *not the potential*, return clearly outweighs the risk. Gambling is very different; it is in favor of the one controlling the game. As they say in Las Vegas, "*They don't pay for the electricity for all those lights by paying out winnings.*" Casinos are in business to make a profit. Any time you place a bet or buy a lottery ticket, the odds are against you.

Purchase a certificate of deposit at a bank. Unlike stocks, this is guaranteed by the federal government up to a specified amount. Typically, this will earn a slightly higher rate of interest than will a savings account.

Purchase real estate. There may be special low down payment and/or low interest loan programs to help first-time buyers, people who have served in the military, teachers, minorities, and other groups. Also, individual homeowners may be willing to allow you to make a monthly payment to them rather than getting a traditional mortgage. This can benefit the buyer and seller in various ways.

If you can't afford to buy, find a home you'd like to own and ask the seller if they'd be willing to lease it to you with an option to buy with a portion of your monthly rent applied toward your sales price. The longer a house has been for sale, the more willing the seller may be to entertain this type of creative arrangement. *Be careful that the seller is not in foreclosure or in risk of losing the house, or you could lose the credit that's being applied.*

If you don't have enough money to buy a house on your own, look for others in your situation who might be willing to be a partner with you. You can buy a property and share the use of it. If that's not feasible, consider finding an investor who could benefit from the tax advantages of a property. If you're able to live in the property, take care of it, and pay the loan, property tax, and insurance payments, the person who puts the down payment on the property gets the benefit of the tax deduction for his or her percentage share of the ownership and his or her share of the appreciation of the property. Later, when you can afford it, you can buy the investor's share; or if the property has increased in value, you can sell the property for a profit for both of you.

BE A FARMER

Like a farmer, wealthy people know how to plant a seed and harvest an entire crop! A farmer can take a relatively small amount of seed and plant it to reap a harvest that weighs literally hundreds of pounds more than the original seed and sells for hundreds of dollars. For example, imagine that the seed was originally worth $5 and the crop that comes from it is worth $500. But if the farmer chooses to grind up his seed and make a few loaves of bread with it rather than use the seed to plant a crop, he will have destroyed all chances of having a large crop that can be sold for much more than the value of the few loaves of bread.

The investor's money is just like the farmer's seed. The investor can take $10 and buy something he wants rather than investing it, but he knows that the smart thing to do is to find a way to turn $100 into $1000. The short-sighted person takes the $100 and buys a pair of shoes that will eventually wear out, or buys a new cell phone that could be lost or stolen, or gets a tattoo that won't help to make money (in fact, the tattoo could wind up keeping him or her from getting a job).

A very basic example would be that if you earn $7 per hour and work a 40-hour week, you earn $280 per week. After taxes, you probably bring home about $196. If you spend $20 each week on food (*yes, it's possible to live on $20 per week*), you'll have $176 left. Multiply this by four weeks in a month, and you have $704 left. If you rent a room or share a place for $500 per month, you have $204 left. If you spend $10 a month on personal items like shampoo, hair spray, toothpaste, etc., (*buying from the 99-Cent Store, getting free samples, and buying with coupons and rebate offers, which often result in items literally costing just pennies*) and $25 per month on a bus pass, that leaves $169 every month that you can save and invest!

If you save $75 per month for a whole year, you will have $900 at the end of the year. At 5 percent interest, you will earn an additional $45, bringing your total to $945. If you did this for five years, you would have almost $5,000 cash! With that money, you could start a business, go in with partners to purchase a small piece of real estate or an asset that will generate income, or make some other investment that could double your money.

You will also reap a bigger harvest and increase your savings if your income increases. While you are working and saving, look for opportunities to make extra money. If you do a good job while you are earning your $7 hourly wage, either your current employer or your future employer or your future business partner will see what you do, how hard you work, and what a good employee you are. As a result, your current employer may offer you additional opportunities to make more money. If you're not offered additional opportunities by your current employer, a future employer or a future business partner may offer you an opportunity that will pay you more than $7 per hour, so your savings will grow at an even faster rate.

This scenario may not represent you at all, but regardless of how much money you earn, the principle is the same. And once you begin to earn more money, continue to live on the amount you're accustomed to earning before your income increased, at least for a while. Save and invest the additional income so that you can gather enough to live the way you really want to live later. Some people relax and quit moving in the direction of their goals as soon as they start making enough money to be slightly comfortable. Don't be one of those people. Continue to live lean and save and invest until the time comes when you can own your own home, drive the car you want to be driving, and live the kind of life you want to be living.

PARTNERS

Some goals cannot be achieved alone. Wealthy people align themselves with partners who have strengths in areas of their weakness. A good partner completes you; they DO NOT compete with you. Partner only with the right people; don't partner with someone who has nothing to offer. Partner with someone who adds something to your goal, such as money, hard work, influence, or a skill, talent, or characteristic that you don't have.

You can have partners in business, in investments, and in other areas of your life. Your "life partner" is your spouse. People also partner to share an apartment, to buy a car, or to start a business. Many people find themselves in partnership with people whom they virtually stumbled into somewhere. Some of those happenstance relationships work out, but many end painfully. Successful people deliberately identify, recruit, and effectively utilize their partners.

In order to make your partnership work, consider your strengths and, perhaps more importantly, your weaknesses. Earlier in this book you spent time considering what you're good at doing. Now think about what you're not very good at doing. Ideally, for a partnership to result in the maximum rewards for everyone concerned, each person should have strengths where the other is weak. In my case, for example, I am a "big picture" person. I want the details accurately and efficiently taken care of, but I'm not a detail-oriented person. So I intentionally surround myself with highly detailed people.

Create a detailed word picture of the perfect partners in life, friendship, and business. What is that person like? What characteristics would make that person perfect? If you're a quiet person who doesn't have a lot of friends, would your perfect partner be someone who is outgoing and makes friends easily? In a business example, if you're someone who is good at bookkeeping, perhaps you would want a business partner to be good at sales.

When you are working with people who are strong in areas where you are weak, disagreements and miscommunications are to be expected. As with any other relationship, when conflict arises, you should:

1. Consider where the other person is coming from.

2. Try to think about how the other person feels.

3. Give the benefit of the doubt about intent and motives.

4. Explain calmly and without anger what you think and feel and why you think and feel that way.

5. Apologize when you've said or done something hurtful.

6. Forgive when you're hurt (whether or not the person asks for forgiveness, whether or not he or she deserves it).

7. Remind your partner that it is natural for two people with different personalities and different skill sets to see things differently. This is part of the benefit of the partnership. For it to work for everyone, though, mutual respect, open communication, and a willingness to resolve conflict and then to MOVE ON is absolutely critical.

Once you've chosen the right partners, it's important to agree on a clear, concise vision of what you mutually want to accomplish. If it's a life partner, decide on the big things, including where you'd like to live, how many kids you want to have, if any, and what kind of involvement you want to have with the other person's family. If it's an investment or business partner, make sure you have clearly defined expectations of everyone involved, a clearly defined mission, a vision for what you want to accomplish, and an estimated time frame for measurement of actual results against goals.

Regardless of what kind of relationship you're partnering in, determine the role of each person. What are each person's responsibilities? What authority does each person have? How do you plan to resolve conflict? What are the consequences of falling short of expectations or failing to perform a responsibility or overstepping one's authority? Clearly communicated expectations will avoid or mitigate problems and pain.

When you think you've found someone you can partner with, whether it is a roommate, a business investment partner, or someone to date, ask yourself if this is a person with integrity. **Do not partner with anyone who has a history of making wrong choices or mistreating people.** Someone who will lie, cheat, or steal will lie to you, cheat on you, and steal from you. People often think, *"I know he cheated on her, but he won't cheat on me."* Remember, a liar lies. A cheater cheats. A thief steals. It's that simple. Avoid pain by avoiding people who have a track record that is not acceptable to you.

PRACTICAL ADVICE FOR KEEPING MORE OF WHAT YOU EARN

Wealthy people pay less for almost everything. Proof of this is everywhere. When a person with cash walks into a car dealership, he or she is able to negotiate a much better price for a car than someone who needs to buy a car on credit. Not only do wealthy people negotiate a lower price for the vehicle, they pay even less because they're not paying interest on a loan. Another illustration of this point would be that a gallon of milk costs much less per ounce than does a half pint of milk. So the person who has enough money to buy the gallon is probably going to pay significantly less per ounce than the person who can only afford a half pint.

What I'm about to tell you in the following sections may seem mundane and simplistic, but I would be remiss if I invested all this time and energy into telling what you should do and then failed to tell you *HOW* to do it. To those who already know what follows, to those who live this way, and to those who have already "paid their

---

Instead of immediately replacing something that breaks, try to repair it.

---

dues" and no longer have to watch every cent, it will seem obvious. Unfortunately, common sense is not so common anymore. In fact, what used to be <u>common</u> sense, meaning that it was commonly known, is now what I call *"uncommon sense"* because it's in rare supply. Even people who are smart, educated adults find themselves struggling financially – some even to the point of filing bankruptcy. Everyone can benefit from getting back to basics and making wise decisions about spending money.

Fix what breaks. After World War II people took a nonworking toaster apart and fixed it, and if that didn't work, they took it to the appliance repair shop, staffed by some old guy who managed to fix nearly every broken thing that walked through the door. Those guys could fix anything. Some of the things we use today can be replaced for less than what it costs to repair them. But there are things we could fix and use a while longer if we'd try.

When I was 16 and freshly emancipated out of the foster care system, I made slightly more than minimum wage, so it was extremely important that I manage what little money I had. I had no choice but to learn how to make my money stretch. Even though I had a very old car that had issues, I knew it would last longer if I took care of it. So I changed my own oil every 3,000 miles without fail; I changed my spark plugs, air filter, and oil filter; and I made sure there was adequate water in the radiator and air in the tires. That car never let me down.

What to do when the best you can do is "get by." I have been well acquainted with Top Ramen, oatmeal, rice, beans, pasta, and peanut butter. I'd make rice or pasta and put whatever I had in the apartment on it – from canned tomato sauce, to frozen vegetables and butter, to a can of chili. No one died from my cooking experiments (*that I know of*), and some of it actually tasted great! When I'd see a fruit tree with limbs full of fruit, I'd stop and ask if I could buy a bag of fruit. Most of the time, people told me to just take what I wanted. Most people can't eat all the fruit on their trees and are happy to give it away rather than see it rot on the ground.

I looked for day old bread, dented cans, and the vegetables, fruit, and meat that had to be eaten that day. Those things were usually half of the original price, and there was nothing wrong with it. Most people don't eat a whole loaf of bread the day they buy it anyway. So the day after they've been to the store, their bread is "day old bread" too. In cultures where people go to open air markets every day to buy food for that day's meal, they often look for the very ripe produce when flavor is at its peak so that they don't have to wait a few days to be able to use it. That's all I was doing – buying today's meal, but at a fraction of the cost that others were paying!

Use a coupon in grocery stores and restaurants. Drink water instead of an overpriced drink. Go to the movies in the afternoon rather than in the evening because the same movie costs less in the afternoon. Watch DVD's at home rather than going to the movies. Sit on the floor with pillows rather than paying for "rent-to-own" furniture, where you wind up paying two to three times what the rented stuff actually costs and is worth.

If you work in an office or retail environment where your appearance can make the difference in commissions, raises, and promotions, save your money and buy a few basic pieces for your wardrobe that are NOT trendy, but classic, so that they can be worn years from now. Buy colors that are basic and that mix well, such as black, white, tan, and navy. Four basic pieces can be combined to make up twelve different outfits! Remember that dark colors don't show dirt, stains, or snags as easily as do lighter colors, and they have the added benefit of making you appear smaller. You can often find professional clothing in excellent condition in consignment stores or online.

Do you buy grocery items at convenience stores or gas stations? You are probably paying two or three times what you would pay at the grocery store or a warehouse-type store. Why buy a bottle of water or a soda for $1.29 when a six-pack at the grocery store is 60 cents each and 45 cents or less when it's discounted?

Do you take your lunch to work? You can buy rice, beans, mac 'n cheese, nuts, trail mix, soup, bread, peanut butter, and other food that is nutritional and filling for just a small amount of money, especially if you can find a 99-Cent Store or something like it. Buy plastic bags or reusable containers so that you can take food to work. If you can find an inexpensive insulated bag to keep the food for your lunch from going bad, that is great. If not, you can get a plastic cup and top, fill it with juice or water, and freeze it the night before. Use this to keep your food cold in a lunch bag. By lunch time, it'll be thawed enough to drink AND will have kept your lunch from spoiling.

If others are going out to lunch, instead of going along and spending money you know you should save, choose to take a walk, take a nap, read a book, listen to music, do extra work, balance your checkbook, write letters, or look through magazines for pictures of the life you want to live and things you want to have.

Don't be afraid of being left out or being alone. Being alone offers an excellent opportunity to keep the end result of your goals in front of you. Typically the people going out to lunch will not be motivated and goal-minded. So, spending your free time with them could possibly distract you from your goals and delay your accomplishments. It's just not worth it.

Even though I now have the means to walk into any grocery store and purchase anything I want without having to check to see how much money I have or whether or not I have a coupon for the item, I still check the price per ounce and buy the better priced and sized product. I take advantage of store sales and purchase things that have been marked down for clearance. *Just because I CAN pay more for an item than what it's worth, doesn't mean I should.* It's never smart to pay too much.

When you eat out, notice the prices of the drinks compared to the food. Many people go for the "$1 menu" and then buy a soda for $2. For the same $3, get three items off the "$1 menu" and drink water. Use a coupon to buy one meal and get the other free. Some places have "early bird" or "happy hour" time frames where the prices of many items are temporarily reduced.

If you purchase a soda or a bottle of water every day for $1 each, you're spending $365 unnecessarily every year. Save money by drinking water from a faucet. This is better for you than sodas because water has no calories; furthermore, it won't ruin your teeth and it is free. Don't buy the myth that you have to be drinking bottled water for it to be good for you. If you're in the United

States, there are strict rules regarding the regulation of the water supply from our faucets and its content. Tap water is fine almost anywhere in the United States. I wonder if some of the bottled water we are buying is nothing more than tap water! For the price of a couple bottles of water, you can probably buy a thermos or a jug, fill it with ice cubes and water for the day, and have cool drinking water all day.

If you get *designer* coffee for $3.50 each four times per week, you're spending $14 per week, which works out to an average of $56 per month. That is $672 per year! Now, I'm not suggesting that you not drink specialty coffee. If you love it and want it, have it; but be smart about it. Buy a bag of specialty or flavored coffee for $9, get a coffee maker for approximately $15 (or much less if you can find one at a yard sale), buy your flavored creamer or syrup at the grocery store for less than $4, and then make coffee every day for a whole month for $28 for the first month and $9 every month thereafter, for a total of $127. This is a savings of $545 in the first year alone.

The designer container and lid doesn't make the coffee taste any better, and carrying a designer cup around doesn't make you look cool. In fact, when I see people carrying a container of coffee they have obviously purchased somewhere, I wonder about their ability to manage money effectively, not to mention their time. In addition to spending the money on gas to drive somewhere to get coffee, there is the issue of waiting in line at the coffee store. I have a coffee maker with a timer on it. I put everything in the night before, set the timer, and the coffee is ready when I roll out of bed in the morning. It's cheap, it takes little time, and it requires no gas. Convenience PLUS money saved is a very good combination!

There were so many other ways that I have stretched money. I learned how to sew and made clothes for my daughter and me. I cut coupons and didn't buy <u>anything</u> that I didn't absolutely need. I would mail in rebate forms and celebrate when the one-dollar rebate would arrive. I saved all my change and exchanged it for paper dollars twice a year. That's the money that went toward car insurance. When I needed a hair cut, I went to the local beauty college and paid a fraction of what others paid at the salon. Because I saved and did without for years, I was able to invest in the businesses and properties that ultimately resulted in the life I have now. Although it's been a long time since I've had to do any of these things, I still use my resources wisely. Regardless of how much money I ever have, I can't imagine every being reckless with it.

CHAPTER 13

ADVICE OF ROLE MODELS

I've given you my advice for determining and achieving your goals and fulfilling your specific purpose in life. But don't just take my word for it. Some of the best advice has come from people who experienced the greatest of successes in their fields. The following bits of advice and much more valuable help can be found on the Internet.

William Raspberry, writer and Pulitzer Prize winner, said, *"If you want to be thought of as a solid, reliable pillar of your community when you're 50, you can't be an irresponsible, corner-cutting exploiter at 25... the time to worry about your reputation is before you have one. You determine your reputation by deciding who and what you are and by keeping that lofty vision of yourself in mind, even when you're having a rip-roaring good time."*

Alan Greenspan, former Chairman of the United States Federal Reserve, said, *"It is decidedly not true that 'nice guys finish last' as that highly original American baseball philosopher, Leo Durocher, was once alleged to have said... I do not deny that many appear* to have succeeded in a material way by cutting corners and manipulating associates, both in their professional and in their personal lives. But material success is possible in this world and far more satisfying when it comes without exploiting others. The true measure of a career is to be able to be content, even proud, that you succeeded through your own endeavors without leaving a trail of casualties in your wake."

Anthony Robbins, motivational speaker and management consultant, said, "Quality questions create a quality life. Successful people ask better questions, and as a result, they get better answers."

When asked about intelligence, Bill Gates, the founder of Microsoft and one of the wealthiest people in the world, said, "Smart is an elusive concept. There's a certain sharpness, an ability to absorb new facts. To walk into a situation, have something explained to you and immediately say, 'Well, what about this?' To ask an insightful question. To absorb it in real time. A capacity to remember. To relate to domains that may not seem connected at first. A certain creativity that allows people to be effective."

David Brinkley, legendary television newsman, said, "A successful person is one who can lay a firm foundation with the bricks that others throw at him or her."

Jack Kerouac, author, said, "… the people who are crazy enough to think they can change the world are the ones who do."

Frank Lloyd Wright, world-renowned architect, said, "I know the price of success: dedication, hard work, and an unremitting devotion to the things you want to see happen."

Abraham Lincoln, perhaps the best President the United States has ever known, said, "Things may come to those who wait, but only the things left by those who hustle."

Ruth Bader Ginsburg, United States Supreme Court Justice, said, "Sometimes people say unkind or thoughtless things, and when they *do, it is best to be a little hard of hearing – to tune out and not snap back in anger or impatience. Anger, resentment, envy, and self-pity are wasteful reactions. They greatly drain one's time. They sap energy better devoted to productive endeavors. Of course it is important to be a good listener – to pay attention to teachers, coworkers, and spouses. But it also pays, sometimes, to be a little deaf."*

Mason Cooley, aphorist, said, *"To be a social success, do not act pathetic, arrogant, or bored. Do not discuss your unhappy childhood, your visit to the dentist, the shortcomings of your cleaning woman, the state of your bowels, or your spouse's bad habits."*

Albert Einstein, physicist, said, *"Try not to become a man of success but rather try to become a man of value."*

Henry Ford, founder of the Ford Motor Company, said, *"Coming together is a beginning; keeping together is progress; working together is success."*

George Adams, musician, said, *"There is no such thing as a 'self-made' man. We are made up of thousands of others. Everyone who has ever done a kind deed for us, or spoken one word of encouragement to us, has entered into the makeup of our character and of our thoughts as well as our success."*

James Cash Penney, founder of J.C. Penney, said, *"Give me a stock clerk with a goal and I'll give you a man who will make history. Give me a man with no goals, and I'll give you a stock clerk."*

Steve Jobs, co-founder and CEO of Apple Computer, said, *"So you've got to have an idea, or a problem, or a wrong that you want to right that you're passionate about otherwise you're not going to have the perseverance to stick it through. I think that's half the battle right there."*

Armand Hammer, founder and president of Occidental Petroleum, said, *"When you work fourteen hours a day, seven days a week, you get lucky."*

Earl Wilson, journalist, said, *"Success is simply a matter of luck. Ask any failure."*

Ralph Waldo Emerson, poet and philosopher, said, *"Enthusiasm is one of the most powerful engines of success."*

Emerson also is attributed to have said, *"To laugh often and much; to win the respect of intelligent people and the affection of children; to earn the appreciation of honest critics and endure the betrayal of false friends; to appreciate beauty; to find the best in others; to leave the world a little better, whether by a healthy child, a garden patch or a redeemed social condition; to know even one life has breathed easier because you have lived. This is the meaning of success."*

And my personal favorite of Emerson's sayings, *"There is nothing capricious in nature, and the implanting of a desire indicates that its gratification is in the constitution of the creature that feels it."* That means that each of us is here for a reason, a specific purpose that is our individual reason for living. Along with the purpose inside of us is the means to accomplish the purpose.

I found all these quotes within a matter of minutes on the Internet. There is so much good advice available to you. Just go to the library, use a computer with Internet access, and search out your own role models. Apply their advice to your life, and don't allow anyone to keep you from your success.

CHAPTER 14

THE PRESENT IS SO GOOD:
IT SOUNDS LIKE I'M LYING, BRAGGING, OR DELUSIONAL!

O nce I began earning more in a month than I had previously made in a year, I began to acquire all the things I wanted, including an 8,000-square-foot mansion on 34 acres in Southern California, a yacht, Mercedes', Ferrari's, and all the other "things" on my list. Once I had all those things, I realized that although they're nice, they don't matter at all. What matters are our relationships.

No one on his or her death bed ever said, *"I sure am comforted by the cars I've driven and the house I live in."* When you're dying, the building that houses the bed (that you'll never rise up out of again) could be a shack. Other than perhaps providing some comfort, the size of your house has no relevance when you're on your way out.

My dear friend and mentor, Corky Kindsvater, retired CEO of Hillview Acres Children's Home, taught me that our relationships are the most important thing in life. Relationship is everything and everything is relationship. Our relationships with the people in our lives matter so much more than anything we acquire, use, or lose. So never, ever damage or destroy a relationship with someone you care about in order to get more money or acquire more "stuff." And above all, NEVER hurt anyone to get something. If you acquire what you want, but hurt someone or lose a good relationship, you're the loser.

The quality of my life now is so good that it amazes me! I married a wonderful man from a big Italian family, and they have warmly embraced me and have provided the family I never had and always longed for. I have honest, sincere friends who can be counted on in any circumstance. My daily life consists of what many people long for. I say all this not to brag, but to point out that if I can go from being a ward of the court, having nothing and no one, to having all this, anyone can have it – assuming you're willing to pay the price to get it. God didn't make deposits into my bank accounts! But what He did do was to provide opportunities. It was up to me to be willing to do my part. The same is true for you.

The best part about the life I live now and the life you can have is that **I now define who I am**. I am *not* defined by what I went through. I am *not* the white trash ghetto girl I once was. I am *not* a dependent of the court. I am *not* the daughter of a criminal or the grandchild of an alcoholic. The people in my life now don't even know those people, so there's no connection or reflection. Neither are you any of the things you've thought of yourself or things other people have thought of you or said about you. Old labels no longer apply to me, and they don't have to characterize you either. But you must make a CHOICE to change your perception of yourself, to figure out who you want to be, and to start acting as though you were that person.

It's important that I give you the whole picture. Living in a nice place, driving nice cars, wearing nice clothes, and having money in the bank doesn't solve every challenge. In some ways, the old problems are replaced by different challenges.

I've learned that having all the necessities and many of the luxuries of life doesn't change the fact that everything doesn't go my way; bad things still happen, and most things are still outside of my control. The difference is that although tires can still go flat and I can still be inconvenienced by the delay, I can now afford to have someone else change my tire rather than getting out on the side of the road on a hot day to change my own tire.

Even now, after all these years since I left that tumultuous environment of my youth, there are still times when my stomach will clench when I hear the sounds that used to precede violence, like a car pulling up in the driveway or a key turning in a lock. Occasionally, I still feel that I'm an unwanted, uninvited outsider. Unless I receive a written invitation with my name on it, I have the vague feeling that I'm imposing myself where I don't belong. Although it's becoming less and less frequent, sometimes I still have the indistinct sense that I don't deserve anything good.

The first forty years of my life felt like a roller coaster ride that never came to a stop. I HATE roller coasters – the clenched stomach, the feel of anticipation, the dread that fills your body, and the adrenalin that is standing ready to flood you as the roller coaster car ticks and clicks straight up to the apex of its track. Then you reach the top and there's a fraction of a moment of hesitation before the car plunges down. You wonder simultaneously: How safe is this? Has anyone ever been seriously injured or killed on this ride? Is this going to screw up my back or neck? Am I going to lose my lunch?

There are times when I used to think, *"I want to get off this ride. Why am I here? I didn't sign up for this!"* I looked for the "chicken exit" of life, but I guess that's suicide, which is quitting, and I'm not wired for that. It takes far more courage to stay on this ride and ride it on out to the end than to try to get off before your turn is up. Besides, those of us who survived crazy, abusive childhoods are **survivors**. It would be ridiculous to survive all that and give up now. Having gone through all we have, we can conquer the rest of life!

Although the life I have now is so good that it is almost like the fairy tale ending of a children's book, I didn't wake up one day to find everything different. That's not real life. Positive change is a process.

You don't just decide to treat people right and make right choices one day, and find everything different the following day. You have to do this Monday, Tuesday, Wednesday, Thursday, Friday, Saturday, and Sunday of every week, of every month, of every year for the rest of your life.

Genuine prosperity is so much more than money.

I have lived dirt poor; I have lived from paycheck to paycheck; and I have lived knowing that if I never earned another paycheck that I have more than enough money to live comfortably for the rest of my life. Even with the challenges that come along with wealth, I can say without hesitation that life is infinitely easier, more pleasurable, and allows for much greater generosity when you have it.

I suspect that many people who read this book will not be willing to do the work necessary to attain their own financial independence. But I've taken the time and written this book for those who will. If you are reading this now and are willing to implement the simple steps and incorporate the advice I've given, you can achieve what

I've achieved and much more. And when you do, please remember to help others who are willing to do the work by showing them how they can help themselves.

When you rise above others, don't do it by compromising your character. Don't stoop so low as to be dishonest, unfair, or immoral, because if you do that, you've missed the whole point. <u>You will have failed</u>, regardless of how much money you earn.

Genuine prosperity is so much more than money. Some of the things that truly count are:

- Fostering good relationships with people who will care about you regardless of what you're able to do for them
- Being loved just as you are
- Having excellent physical health
- Having faith in God and seeing His goodness in your life
- Having a good attitude
- Enjoying life
- Knowing your purpose and living it
- Having a hope for the future
- Sharing with others less fortunate than you
- Having the sense of fulfillment that comes from an honorably earned paycheck and a job well done

Genuine prosperity certainly can include financial success, but only if you are also enjoying excellent health, peace, fun, laughter, and great relationships with family and friends.

CHAPTER 15

CONCLUSION

Well, now I have told you I changed my life and how you can implement positive change in your own life. If you choose NOT to take these steps, ask yourself why. Do you lack discipline? Are you afraid to fail? Are you afraid of what will change if you succeed? Are you afraid of looking foolish? If so, break that down. Who is going to make fun of you? People who have achieved success? No.

If people ridicule you, it's probably because they haven't achieved success, and they don't want you to have it either. The old saying, "Misery loves company," is true. Most people who will criticize your attempts to improve your circumstances will not even be aware of the fact that they're trying to pull you down and keep you on or below their level. But that is the truth. They don't want you to improve because it will make them feel bad. They may be afraid your relationship will change. They may be afraid that they will no longer be able to control you. Whatever the reason, don't allow anyone to hold you back. The people in your life who genuinely care about you will want you to "go for it," and they'll celebrate with you when you succeed.

People, relationships, and things in our lives are reflections of what we believe. Will you choose to believe that what I have told you really works? If not, I challenge you to suspend your disbelief for a reasonable period of time and give these concepts a chance.

Whatever you want to do with your life, whatever your ultimate goals are, there WILL be a price to pay in the time you will have to invest and the work you will have to do. Notice that I say "invest" and not "spend." That's intentional. The time it takes to complete a class, to read a "how to" book, or to learn from someone online or in person is not time "spent" as much as it is time "invested." That investment will pay off for you when you find the employer who needs those skills you've learned or when you open your own business and serve the clients who need to have done what you know how to do.

By this time you may be thinking this all sounds like too much work. It is a lot of work, but consider your alternatives. You can:

- Just "*get by*" in mediocrity for the rest of your life.

- Struggle financially and emotionally when you're 30, 40, 50, 60…

- Choose immoral, unethical, or illegal activity until you get caught or killed.

- Go from one low-paying job to welfare and then onto the next low-paying job… like my grandfather. He died broke in a run-down hospital where many people wouldn't have left their dog. There was no money even for a funeral. And he was such a miserable person that no one would've come to his funeral anyway.

- Try what I suggest here until it works for you. Then live the life you've designed and have what you want.

Which one of these options do you choose? It's your call. It seems pretty clear cut to me. What do you have to lose in trying what I'm suggesting? Imagine what people will say when they see you succeed – rolling up for a visit in your dream car, wearing the clothes and shoes you want to wear, telling about the job you have, the company you own, where you live, and how happy you are with your life.

Think it can't happen? Well, that's exactly what happened for me. A few years after I started my own business, I moved to an affluent area that just happened to be above where my old boss lived. Every day I would drive past his house as I went to and from work. As my brand new Porsche would roll past his house, I would often think of the day he laughed at me, fully expecting and predicting that I would fail. In hindsight, I'm glad he ridiculed me because it motivated me to get up every day and push through everything that stood between the way things were and the way I wanted things to be. Hearing him and others like him say "*I told you so*" was not an option.

I am not saying it's easy. It's not. It's just that the alternatives are far more painful than doing the work necessary to make your dreams a reality. And the payoff for what I'm suggesting is infinitely greater than the end result of any of the other alternatives. In order to work through all the difficulties that will inevitably come your way as you work the principles I'm giving you, you have to DECIDE to survive the pain you'll feel. You have to RESOLVE that you WILL be successful. If you do that, you will eventually have the life you desire!

If you choose to quit and give up entirely, don't hate or envy people like me who will never give up pursuing our goals and who eventually, inevitably obtain the things we work toward. When you allow yourself to feel hate or jealousy, what you are really doing is telling everyone around you that you're a victim. If you quit and give up, you are not a victim, you are a quitter. Becoming successful is no one's responsibility but yours.

Are you serious about success? If so, then stop wasting your precious time and prepare and position yourself to reach your goals. You may be saying, *"But you don't know my circumstances. You don't know how hard I have it."* No, I don't. But I know that I've experienced some very tough times that were very unfair. I had to do far more than some to get what I have. But I was determined to succeed. If you have the physical and mental ability, there is no valid excuse for accepting failure.

Are you serious about success?

If you will do what I am recommending here, you will begin, very soon, to see the results. When those results start to materialize in your life, you will automatically start feeling better. Anytime we begin to see things looking up and goals that we have worked for start to become a reality, we start to feel better about our situations. When this happens, KEEP DOING THE WORK. Don't do what a lot of people do and stop. If you will keep doing the work, you will continue to get better and better results! In fact, it will no longer be work. Achieving your goals will come so naturally to you that it will be a way of life. If you make a commitment to do what I'm suggesting for even thirty days, you'll begin to see the difference in your life. What have you got to lose?

I know what it's like to start with literally nothing. It doesn't matter where you are starting or how many times you have failed. Until now, you might not have had the one piece of the puzzle that was going to be *just the thing* that resulted in reaching your goals.

A lot of people caution others not to get their hopes up. But I recommend you get them up just as high as you can! It may appear that there is no possible way for your situation to ever improve. But the truth is that if you're reading this, things can change. The key to making the change is that we have to be willing to do something. You have to be willing to do work that you really don't want to do, to help someone and expect nothing in return, to work for less money than you think you deserve, or to sacrifice some other way. When we stretch ourselves to prepare for success and take the leap of faith, we open ourselves up to new possibilities.

I look forward to hearing about YOUR success!

SUGGESTED READING

The Bible (I like the Amplified and New American versions best) – *special emphasis on the book of Proverbs for timeless wisdom and advice*

Think and Grow Rich, Napoleon Hill

The Law of Success, Napoleon Hill

The Power of Positive Thinking, Dr. Norman Vincent Peale

See You at the Top, Zig Ziglar

The Power of Agreement, Brian Molitor

Miracles Can Be Yours Today, Pat Robertson

Man's Search for Meaning, Viktor Frankl

Rich Dad, Poor Dad, Robert Kiyosaki

Cradles of Eminence, Victor and Mildred Goertzel

The Mary Kay Way, Mary Kay Ash

Positivity, Dr. Barbara Fredrickson

Strengths Finder 2.0, Tom Rath